# THE FA
# HA

## Sixty years in cattle markets and the history of Wright-Manley from 1860

## A personal account

### by

# BRIAN PENNINGTON

### Cheshire Country Publishing, Chester

ISBN 0 949001 19 8

First published in the United Kingdom in 2002
by Cheshire Country Publishing

# Contents

# Acknowledgements

I have recognised the help I have received in writing this book from most of the undermentioned in the appropriate chapters. However, I feel that an extra word of thanks in the preface is called for.

Firstly, to Mr Frank Young, in his centenary year at the time of writing, for information on Henry Manley & Sons Ltd. detailed in an old letter.

To Mr Fred Wright for his contribution regarding his late father, Leonard, and the firm he established – Leonard Wright & Co.. To Mr George Ford, of Manley Hall, and Mr Leigh Sadler, of Aldersey, Chester, for additional information on the former partners and staff of Leonard Wright & Co., at Chester Smithfield.

To Mr Alan Wright, for providing details of early family tracings and confirmation of correct details in some 'grey areas' of my research, and also for providing several photographs. To Mr Ted Hewitt, of Eaton, Tarporley, for providing copies of early press cuttings and detailed information on the Hewitt family.

To the Wright family and the successive partnerships for providing me with a lifetime's work.

To all the characters featured in the book who have provided the raw material for the text.

To Mr Gordon Davies, of Crewe, for his photographs and comments. To Mr Malcolm Scott, the present Company Secretary of Wright-Manley, for providing material which 'came his way' during the course of his employment with the firm.

To anybody who has been unintentionally omitted from these few words of market history, I apologise beforehand. Due to the large number of people who I have had the pleasure of meeting, and dealing with during the course of my career, it would be virtually impossible to remember them all. Suffice it to say that the characters and personalities featured in this book are a truly representative cross-section.

To Mrs Jen Cox, of Chapel-en-le-Frith, for her endless patience and invaluable assistance in typing and retyping the manuscripts.

To Mark Bevan, of Cheshire Country Publishing, for all his encouragement and guidance during the course of publication. Without his support my literary efforts would never have come to fruition.

To Roger Morris, formerly of Llanarmon-yn-Iâl, a past member of staff who I met again by chance in the latter stages of my first attempt to 'write a book'. His assistance in slotting together a somewhat complex history, which I have obtained from a variety of sources, has been invaluable. Finally, there are many members of staff, past and present, whom I have had the privilege of working with, but have found it impractical to mention. The great majority were a pleasure to work alongside and their efforts and enthusiasm have helped to make the company what it is today.

**BRIAN PENNINGTON**

# Foreword

Brian Pennington has lived, worked and played in Cheshire all his life. I first met him and his late wife, Margaret, many years ago through our mutual interest in Shetland ponies. It soon became apparent to me that here was a man who loved the countryside and all aspects of it, enjoyed his work and was, above all, a people's man.

During his lifelong connection with Wright-Manley, whose history is well documented from its beginnings through to Beeston becoming one of the largest and most important Livestock Centres in England, Brian has met and known countless thousands of country folk, farmers and dealers.

This book contains many of the quite amazing tales relating to such people, as well as interesting stories of himself.

From the Cattle Markets of Crewe, Chester, Beeston and beyond, from specialist cattle sales to horse sales, from Foot & Mouth times to, yes, greyhounds, agricultural and implement sales, the author tells a lifetime's story from his sixty-five years' involvement.

A Professional Auctioneer, famed for his deep voice, friendship and a glint in his eye, his memories and experiences, mixed with important pieces of history, are now preserved for all time.

Today he enjoys a happy and well deserved retirement with his family and second wife, Betty, spending time both in his much-loved Cheshire countryside and at the Fylde coast.

A season ticket holder, he rarely misses watching his beloved Crewe Alexandra, of which some of the Football Club's early days are carefully written.

Yet Brian has found time to write a book of such great interest to a wide variety of people and supported by over eighty photographs...and it is all linked in one way or another to THE FALL OF THE HAMMER!

DAVID KAY
Past President of the National Shire Horse Society

# Introduction

The word 'auction' means increase and was first used in the 16th Century for selling, by means of increasing bids, as against the Dutch method of decreasing bids. Some auctions were controlled by the burning of a short candle. Timing of the bid was crucial, as the sale was over when the flame went out.

Items are sold for the highest offer, unless this is below a reserve price, which is set by the vendor. The auctioneer takes a percentage from the seller or buyer – sometimes from both. It is usually illegal for sellers to bid for their own lots in order to increase the price; and for 'rings' of dealers to keep prices down. One of the first and best-known auctions was created by a Lancashire born man named Mr Richard Tattersall, who started an auction of thoroughbred horses in the 18th Century, which remains in operation at Newmarket, in Cambridgeshire, to this day.

The inspiration of putting pen to paper has developed during retirement, when one begins to realise that at 75 years of age, you are old enough to have heard of the beginning and still young enough to remember the 65 years of personal experience that you have in store. What is to follow (before it is too late – eroded by death and the destruction of evidence) is a record of how cattle markets started off, progressed and developed until the present time.

The evolution of regional auctioneers over the past century and a half sprang from business people who raised the auction system to life, on the basis that an auctioneer must be honest, and show fairness to both buyer and seller. This service to the farming community has provided a barometer to the livestock trade, comparable to the 'Stock Exchange' in the City. It will be to the detriment of Livestock Farming interests if it does not receive the future support to which it is entitled, in order to maintain a true reflection of supply and demand in an up-to-the minute situation.

By including some of my personal experiences and weaving them in to the text to add a little more interest, I will hopefully portray the times through which the reader will pass; before technology obliterates the characters the livestock auction system produced.

Accordingly, as Wright-Manley was created from three separate enterprises, it would seem a sensible literary route to write the history of these companies, families and partnerships, under separate chapters. Because Crewe is my home town and the market where my interests were first kindled, there is no better place for the story to begin.

*Beeston Castle Smithfield from the air in the 1980's.*

# CHAPTER ONE
## Crewe Cattle Market

The Livestock Auction system evolved from the age-old practice of private barter. Cattle fairs at Crewe were no exception, in as much as these fairs started along with the general development of Crewe as a railway town, in the centre of an area heavily populated with livestock.

The first fairs were held in the town centre, behind the Adelphi Hotel, which is now a mobile phone shop, and gradually spread into the adjacent streets in about 1850, when five fairs were held each year. As it grew in popularity, the Cattle Fair became a monthly event and also a major political issue; with the townspeople objecting to the accompanying filth and pollution. Nevertheless, Cattle Fairs continued in the town until 1896.

The first auction sale was held on March 2nd, 1874, by Mr William Hill, in a field behind the Royal Hotel, which was owned at that time by Mr Charlie Welch, a prominent local dignitary. These sales were held initially on a monthly basis, then due to the advantage of the proximity of the site to the Railway Station, they quickly became a weekly event and attracted the interest of local investors.

Accordingly, the Crewe Cattle Market and Abattoir Company was

*The beginnings of Crewe Railway Station, 1848, and showing, in the middle of the photograph, the old Locomotive Works.*

*Frank Webb (right), the uncrowned 'King of Crewe', Chief Mechanical Engineer, Crewe Railway Works, 1836-1906, with foreign visitors about to board the observation car for a 'works tour'. Frank Webb was one of the backers of the first market.*

formed in 1882 and included directors of the London & North Western Railway Company. A new market, consisting of lairages, sale rings and a slaughter-house, was built on land leased from the railway company, operating on a commission levy of 2d (old pence) in the £ (240d). Rail access was made available through a siding to the Gresty Road site from the Main Junction and was opened in 1883 with the blessing and support of such men as Sir Richard Moon and Frank Webb, who were pioneers of the railway network in Great Britain.

The first auctioneers to this company were Messrs J.C. & H.H.Etches. However, it would appear that the company had taken steps, possibly too ambitious for the time, and were also handicapped by outbreaks of Foot & Mouth disease. As a result, the market was leased to Messrs Etches and Mr Henry Manley, who was already conducting livestock sales at Whitchurch and Wrenbury.

Henry Manley was born at Aston in 1828, the son of a wheelwright,

8

and became the village postmaster, general dealer and chemist. He held his first auction at Aston, near Nantwich, in 1861 in what was claimed to be the first purpose-built livestock market in Cheshire. It was adjacent to the Salamanca Hotel which is now closed, although part of the market office still remains to this day – more about Wrenbury later.

In 1895, the company terminated the agreement at Crewe with Messrs Etches and Manley, who by this time had built up a thriving market and, without consulting either Etches or Manley, leased the market to Mr Frank Lloyd, of Wrexham. Henry Manley, therefore decided to build his own market on the other side of Gresty Road, namely 'The Middle Market', which opened in February 1896. After continuing to build on his previous success he died in 1903 and was buried in Aston Cemetery, on September 24th, leaving four sons who had been made partners in the business in 1900, when Messrs Henry Manley & Sons Ltd. was first formed.

Cattle Market number three was erected shortly after the Middle Market by Messrs J.M. Barker & Co who also held a market at Northwich. Frank Lloyd, of Wrexham, subsequently took the lease of the Gresty Road Market and so the scene was set for three livestock auctions competing against each other.

My first awareness of a Cattle Market in Crewe was in the early 1930's, when it stems quite vividly from my boyhood memories, that the last thing to be done on a Sunday evening was to close the garden

*Henry Manley with his four sons.*

9

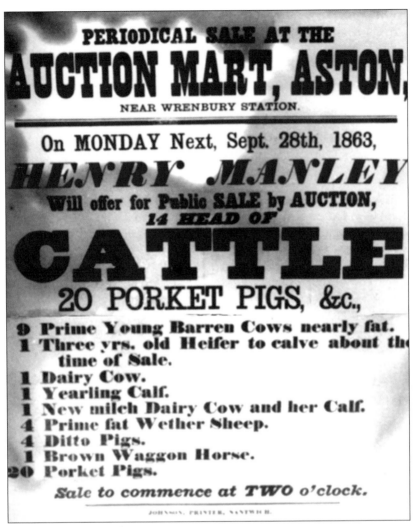

**PERIODICAL SALE AT THE**

# AUCTION MART, ASTON,

### NEAR WRENBURY STATION.

## On MONDAY Next, Sept. 28th, 1863,

# HENRY MANLEY

**Will offer for Public SALE by AUCTION,**

## 14 HEAD OF

# CATTLE

## 20 PORKET PIGS, &c.,

**9 Prime Young Barren Cows nearly fat.**
**1 Three yrs. old Heifer to calve about the time of Sale.**
**1 Dairy Cow.**
**1 Yearling Calf.**
**1 New milch Dairy Cow and her Calf.**
**4 Prime fat Wether Sheep.**
**4 Ditto Pigs.**
**1 Brown Waggon Horse.**
**20 Porket Pigs.**

### Sale to commence at TWO o'clock.

JOHNSON, PRINTER, SANDWICH.

*One of the first sales at Cheshire's first Auction Mart.*

gate of our small town home, against all classes of livestock, which would be driven along to the Gresty Road Centre during the early hours of Monday morning. I was the son of a third generation railwayman and never recall any complaints from either my own family, or any others that this droving practice was a nuisance or inconvenience.

By that time it was accepted as part of the business of the town, and that we were fortunate to have its spin-off value in the way of employment and business. In fact, it was a weekly task to shovel the resultant manure into Mother's bucket for the benefit of Father's allotment for which he was always grateful. How attitudes were to change in years to come, when we had so many complaints from local residents, about the noise and smell of livestock which emanated from the market.

As a 'railway boy' I was reared to the 'buzzer' – a local alarm system operated by the railway company, through a steam siren, which prompted its 10,000 workers to be punctual. It started at 7:45 am with three blasts, 7:50 am, 7:55 am and 8:00 am – last clock time no buzzer. Arrive at 8:05 am – lose 15 minute's pay; 8:10 am – lose half an hour's pay; 8:15 am – lose one hour's pay; 8:16 am – no work – gates locked! A similar system operated at dinner time when one hour was allocated for lunch. The men, Father and Grandfather included, ran home to a cooked meal, and then ran back to work again within the hour. These were times when most townspeople had nothing; some had a little; burglaries were rare and the front door key hung on a piece of string in the letterbox. So different to life in 2002.

My second agricultural connection was to spread manure for Mr Ted Smith, of Vine Tree Farm, Wistaston (now Dane Bank College). It had been moved by horse-drawn cart from the midden in the farmyard, to the butt tops in the field, at a rate of 10 rucks per load, 10 yards between rucks, and 100 rucks per acre. The pay was 5 shillings per acre, and the skill at which I became very adept helped me develop, to some extent, the physique required to withstand and survive the rough and tumble of life as a child in a railway town.

In turn, this connection was to introduce me to other general farm duties including milking by hand. Also, I was a milk round assistant when doorstep deliveries were made to the jug, direct from 10-gallon tankards transported by pony and float. The milk often included some chance cigarette ash and other foreign bodies, which nobody ever seemed to get very excited about. Seasonal duties in lofts, threshing boxes and root fields came and went; and then a milestone when I had to assist in driving three roan Irish heifers from the market, via Bedford Street and Nantwich Road, to Vine Tree Farm.

By this time I would be all of ten-years-old and must have been infected by the market bug, as the next experience I remember was a visit to Gresty Road, from Edleston Road School, to the Noted Horse Repository (Manley's Auction); the premises in the middle yard, which served to duplicate for the sale of Irish cattle on Mondays.

Here I was to witness, in amazement, the private negotiations which were taking place, no doubt following a failed attempt to find a buyer in the sale ring. The horse for sale was trotted out and galloped back, led and backed, accompanied by oaths and curses. Hands half met until the price gap was closed and the final deal was done with one almighty slap of the hand. There were few written conditions in those days – a man's word was his bond, his eyes were his judge, his pocket his guide and his money the last thing to part with!

This particular deal took place on the 'stones' outside the market office. The buyer turned to the boy who had witnessed the transaction with the words 'Dos't want a job lad?' 'Yes please,' I replied. 'Then take this (a huge dapple grey gelding) to Church Farm, Wistaston'. I am sure I grew an inch as I took the white halter to lead this magnificent beast under the archway to Gresty Road. The nearest route was down Bedford Street, but Brian wanted as many people – especially school pals – to see his charge and proceeded along South Street to Nantwich Road. By today's standards there was virtually no traffic, but the first bus put Neddy on two hind legs and Brian off both feet clinging to the end of the halter, wishing he'd taken the quiet route! I hung on, and passed Edleston Road as proud as a peacock and, eventually, walked my gelding into Church Farm.

Here I was met by Stan Crewe who thanked me and gave me half a crown! I couldn't believe such money could be earned for so little effort, and I ran the two miles home clutching the silver coin and presented it to my Mother. On reflection I am sure the animal could have been delivered by wagon for a similar fee, but knowing Stan in later years he was a generous man and I had been paid on the right side of the Royal Hotel!

# CHAPTER TWO
## Henry Manley & Sons Ltd.

By 1930 Crewe Auction had established itself as the largest and, arguably, the most important livestock centre in England. As a result of the Manley enterprise, the three markets – Gresty Road, the Middle Market and Barker Street – were operating under the banner of Henry Manley & Sons Limited. The company chairman was Mr Ernest Wright, who had defected from Frank Lloyd & Sons to join the Manley family. The directors also included Mr E.S. Millard,

*Ernest Wright in the market office.*

Nantwich (Furniture and Property), Mr F. Manning, Crewe (Accounts), along with Robert and Hugh Manley.

The firm also had branches in Whitchurch, Nantwich and Market Drayton, with smaller markets at the first and last, plus a prestigious office for pedigree livestock exports, in Southampton Row, London. The weekly market for all commercial stock was held every Monday, whilst the very name became synonymous with the sales of pedigree livestock of all classes, and was recognised both nationally and internationally as a firm of high repute. They also acted as secretaries to several breed societies, including the North West British Friesian Society, Yorkshire Pedigree Pig Breeders, and Cheshire (Crewe) Pedigree Pig Breeders Clubs; also the Pedigree Shorthorn Society.

Henry Manley & Sons Ltd. had also become a household name through the renowned Horse Sales and I well remember a picture of the Horse Repository with the supporting caption 'Crewe Autumn Foal Sales 1,300 in two days'. Hackney Sales attracted entries nation-wide; and Greyhound Sales were a regular Saturday fixture.

Crewe, favoured by its railway communications, was second only to Peterborough for the sale of high class Shire Horse breeding stock and, in terms of sheer numbers sold, it was outstanding. Henry Manley & Sons Ltd. had opened their new repository in 1901 with a three-day sale of 750 horses. A special train-load of geldings which left for London at 5.20pm arrived at 9.20pm on the same day. The railway siding from the main junction, which had been keyed directly to the Gresty Road end, was almost in daily use, whilst another dock was available for cattle vans and horse boxes in Tommy's Lane, adjacent to the Crewe Arms Hotel.

HENRY MANLEY & SONS, LTD.
Auctioneers, Valuers and Shippers of Pure-bred Live Stock,
LONDON & CREWE.
will conduct sales as follows :—
COLLECTIVE FRIDAY, JULY 19th, at CREWE,
CATTLE Sale of GUERNSEY and JERSEY
NOTE :—Special Entries should be notified at once.
MANLEY'S accommodation is now provided at
making it the REPOSITORY, CREWE, for T.T. Cattle,
PREMISES IN THE BRITISH LIVE STOCK SALE
finest up-to-date
ROYAL SHOW, Newcastle,
JULY 2nd to 6th.
Our usual Business Bureau will be at Stand 338
Avenue J, when our Expert Service will be available for
both Home and Overseas Trade. A Number of the stock
exhibited will be placed in our hands for sale. An Expert
from our Estate Dept. will also be in attendance to give
advice on Agricultural Properties.
Correspondence to HENRY MANLEY AND SONS,
LTD. "SENTINEL HOUSE," SOUTHAMPTON ROW,
LONDON, W.C.1. Tel. : Holborn 9200; and CREWE,
Tel. : 2654, who will execute commissions.

Press cutting from ex-Farmer and Stock Breeder', June 1935.

The Irish connection was also in full swing and made good use of the Port of Holyhead. The reader can, to some extent, perhaps visualise the atmosphere that was generated and the hubbub that ensued when one considers the business activities which took place on this 2.5 acres of land.

It comprised four sale rings and a slaughter-house; accommodation for hundreds of sheep, pigs, and home bred dairy cattle; together with lorry wash facilities, furniture store, snack bar and restaurant, offices, shops, and corn merchants stands. The whole road frontage was sealed by stockproof iron gates and railings 15 feet high, with the company's offices (which also housed the Market Foreman, Mr Walter Welch and his family), built in best Ruabon brick to impress potential buyers arriving by either road or rail. On sale days that part of Crewe would vibrate with the clatter of hooves and the bellowing of cattle. The sale rings would be crowded with experienced buyers and sellers, drovers, clerks and auctioneers. There would be considerable noise, laughter, rivalry and comradeship.

The site of Crewe Cattle Market is now the extended new stand and car park for Crewe Alexandra F.C.. I first attended Gresty Road with my Grandfather and well remember one of my first unaccompanied

*The first Crewe Alexandra stand burned down in 1932.*

visits, when I was allowed to go with my cousin, Bill Parratt, to watch the Alex versus Sheffield Wednesday, in a cup-tie, in about 1935. We were in the boys' seats, a plank at the edge of the pitch where the Bluebell Stand is now sited, and we were warned to wait until the crowd had left before making our own exit – we left it so long, we were locked in!

No supporters of those years – when the urine trickled along Gresty Road, through the rusty steel sheets that formed the boundary fence and toilet – would ever have dreamed that Gresty Road could possibly have been developed into the stadium it is today. It is of great credit to the present manager and directors who deserve increased support from the football supporters in the area.

*Dario Gradi, Crewe Alexandra's long-serving Manager,*
*arrives at Gresty Road.*

15

In those halcyon days, before marketing groups were even heard of, or direct sales were ever considered, a man could earn a living from twenty acres, or less. Our part of the country could absorb dairy cattle in plenty to supply milk to the big conurbations through those who specialised in obtaining stock from the rearing grounds of the North and elsewhere. Names, some long forgotten, like Charlie Hancock, Hughie Williams, Fred Robinson, John Goddard, Bob Faulkner, Mark Baker and Johnny Goodall etc., all 'stood the market' every Monday, each with their own shippon or bay. Only the first two families survive in the business today, whilst Peter Faulkner, Violet Salmon and Arthur Robinson will each have their own particular memories of that era.

In the Dairy Ring, the auctioneer was Wilf Barnes (son of the Duke of Westminster's Head Gardener). I well remember listening to Ted Smith's account of how the late Norman Callwood, of Rope, had made a spectacle of himself by purchasing an animal for a £20 bid in the ring, purely to draw attention to himself; no farmer could pay that sort of money and survive! Norman recently passed away at the age of 94 after a long and successful life as a dairy farmer.

The odd calf shown with its dam would often be purchased by Tom Moss, Remer Street, Coppenhall, complete with rose in buttonhole and turned out to such a high standard of appearance as would befit today's wedding guest. Most market men were always turned out well by their devoted wives to at least start the day in smart attire, clean slops, polished boots, leggings and so on.

*Cheshire farmers 'at play' in a cricket knockout in 1922.*

*Ernest Wright in the cattle pens with Alec Furber*
*(with cap) in the background.*

Another few yards and you were in the fat cattle ring with auctioneers John Bourne and David Wright (Ernest Wright's son who was killed in Egypt during the war) where prominent butchers of the day competed fiercely to source their weekly requirements, including such names as Barlows, Fittons, Pickups and various heads of Co-op's. Cruising between them for support would be prominent men like the Hollands, of Northwich, with an interest in many of the lots to be sold. Family feuds often prevailed by clashes in personality and envy and I remember the story of a Barlow approaching a Fitton at one of the Christmas Sales in those days, and in an attempt to reach an amnesty to the expensive sale ring battles which had prevailed for a long time prior – hand outstretched, said, 'It's Christmas Sid, let us forgive and forget?' To which Sid replied, 'I shall forgive, but I shall never ever forget!' Company mergers and take-overs became inevitable changes in what was then often an extended family structure.

Rostrums in the other sale rings were occupied by part time auctioneers, Frank Bather, of Ellesmere, and Mr (Winkey) Vernon, of Audlem; the former with a delivery like a machine gun, and the latter who preached like a poet. The pig specialist was Thomas Horton Jefferson, a man who had a natural ability and foresight in the livestock marketing world, and played a significant role as a 'backroom boy' in the development of Crewe Market, which was never fully appreciated or recognised.

The Youngs, of Wistaston; Frank Furber, of Austerson; and others provided the bulk of the sheep entries, which they had mainly imported from the North of England. The Young family also provided the last managing director of Messrs Henry Manley & Sons Ltd., namely Mr Frank Young who, at 99 years of age, is still alive at the time of writing, and has been extremely helpful in compiling this publication.

Now we move over Gresty Road and under the archway to the Middle Yard (the Irish Section) to be solicited by either the Kerrys or the Keenans, the Dales, the Davieses or the Donavons, the Byrnes or George Brazenhall, Sam Loundes, Johnny Ellis or the Fords – all trying to sell one or more of the Reds and Roans, Blues, Blacks or Whites imported from Ganley's, of Dublin, during the previous week.

Through to the stables and horse 'rings', which were oblong in shape with a sleepered run from the buyers' covered area and rostrum out into the open – where the exhibitor would walk a newly shod workhorse out and trot it back with a noise like thunder as the irons hit the sleepers – then back into the sales area. A common call I remember from Ernest Wright...

'Take her down again Darkie and I'll sell 'er when she comes back!'

And finally, we cross over to the Barker Street Market which had been named after the auctioneer of that name, Massey Barker who held sales in the galvanised iron, dome-topped sheds, but was less

*Three boy drovers – l-r, Vincent Wakeley, Jack Morris and Gordon Davies, with Tom Farrall.*

18

successful in his efforts to tap the livestock resources of the area than either Manley's or Lloyd's. This west wing was now used on Mondays for extensive calf sales and on other days for accredited dairy cattle sales of different breeds, including Channel Island cattle from Mr Robert Eddy, of Cornwall; and Ayrshires from Tommy Bell and Johnstons, from Scotland. Cattle wagons holding six to ten cows were replacing drovers and the local hauliers – Haydons, of Biddulph; Dales, of Smallwood; Boltons, of Hassal Green; and Atkinsons, of Wybunbury – served most areas.

It also provided a living for garages and drivers in each village. How would Jimmy Leech of Haslington ever have tolerated a tachograph, or Ernie Ash (Congleton), Bill Broster (Moston), Vic Espley (Arclid), Sandersons, Joe Moss, Geoff Pass, Bert Cranston, Dodd, Partons, Dakins, Hewitts and Dick Manley – just a few from the Crewe side? A mere handful service the county for today's requirements with outfits moving up to forty cows at a time.

A cattle market in a town always generated a wealth of casual employment and in the hard times of the 1930's and early 1940's when large families struggled to exist, Crewe Auction was a haven of comparable prosperity for schoolboys who lived in the adjoining streets. I had now become recognised as a school holidays' boy drover and would court the favour of Mr Walter Welch to be taken on, along with other casuals from the station who would work foreigners from the LMS & P.Way. I was usually allocated to the beef lairage with other drovers who had names like Bottles, Darkie, Budge Cook, Jimmy Povell, Fred Woolley and Wilmot Welch.

After the sale was over, which entailed about six hours work, one reported to Mr Welch for a pay chit which simply read – '2 shillings, W. W. Hence'. At the office the 'rags and tags' from other sections were mustering for payment. It was nothing to wait an hour, or two, before Mr Fred Manning would consider opening his cash till for payout and it was a lively scene when some of the drovers (who were used to and expected delays) would return from the Royal Hotel, The Barrel or 'The Pig' on Nantwich Road, and either break into song, or become aggressive – it was all part of the Monday scene!

Whole families benefited, including the Belchers, whose mother produced twenty children, many of whom found employment as drovers at Gresty Road and one in particular, namely Wilf, who was to be appointed Market Foreman in the ensuing years. Then there was the Davies and Robinson families who, in later years, established themselves as cattle dealers and traders in their own right.

19

*Frank Blunstone who started his football career on the market paddock with 'Gates for Goalposts' became a schoolboy international and went on to play for 'The Alex', Chelsea and England.*

Other family names who were introduced into rural life were the Dyers and the Blunstones, who succeeded not only as drovers, but also as professional footballers, through the adjoining premises on Gresty Road – Crewe Alexandra Football Club. Both Alec Dyer and Frank Blunstone reached the highest levels of their day and were selected to play for Scotland and England respectively, an amazing accomplishment from those early connections.

What a contrast of facilities for the training of young footballing prospects. Crewe Auction Horse Paddock with gateposts for goal posts, compared to the new complex for the Football Academy at Reaseheath, near Nantwich!

*Alec Dyer (left), 'Market-bred' footballer who played for 'The Alex', Aberdeen, Plymouth FC and was capped for Scotland as a guest in wartime international matches, seen here with Ernie Tagg (centre), former Crewe Alex. FC Manager, and Stanley Mortenson, England international, Blackpool etc..*

20

# CHAPTER THREE
## 1939-1945 The Second World War

In 1937, I moved from Edleston Road Primary School where I began my education, along with Reg Beard, of Balterley, and Geoff Holland, of Hassall, amongst many others, and on to Crewe Grammar School. Then, in 1939, the 'Outbreak of War' was to change many things and many people; boys became men very quickly, and I continued my association with the market by obtaining weekend work with the Keenans in the Irish cattle section. The routine was briefly as follows:

> **Stage 1.** Friday pm or Saturday am – unload ten to twenty Shorthorn cattle off the railway sidings, their 'bellies up their backs' after a long rail and sea journey, looking very bedraggled, dirty and ready for a rest on the beds of deep, clean straw.
> The Irish remedy for reviving these cattle was a good feed of fresh hay and bran mash which was scalded in old cheese vats with boiling water, then carried to them in buckets until they could eat no more, after which they were all milked by hand.

> **Stage 2.** Saturday morning – milked (stripped) five times, washed, horns sawn and reshaped with a 'pulling knife'. Age rings removed by rasp followed by a finer file to reveal a gleaming white horn, polished and topped with a sparkle from the wax readily available in the animal's ear hole.

> **Stage 3.** More bran mash, clipped tails and back (my job to wind the clipper handle), groomed, tail ends fluffed with currycombs and cow cards.

It was at this point that, to the amusement of our Irish employers and other market men who happened to be there, we had our monthly appointment with the 'hairdresser'.

The same cow clippers were used to give us boys a 'close crop'. This was to ensure that the lice we had acquired from the cow, via our milking position (head in flanks to stop a kicker), was reduced to a minimum and the insects had no room to work. We were the original skin heads!

**Stage 4.** Final stripping on Sunday morning, more bran mash and rest.

**Stage 5.** Monday morning before school – 'red raddle the udders'! A beast had been transformed from an animal almost unsaleable in appearance, to a show cow in forty-eight hours. Cows with eight calf wrinkles made to look like second calvers! I wonder where the 'Office of Fair Trading Standards' would have fitted into a system regulated by four words – Caveat Emptor – "Let the buyer beware!"

**Stage 6.** Pay – ten shillings plus milk, which was now rationed along with every other commodity! Mother acquired a small glass butter churn, which provided us with an extra supplement to the week's food.

1942 - From an early age I always had the Royal Navy in mind as a career; no doubt influenced by my uncle, (a bachelor sailor), who

*The Beauty Parlour – the removal of wrinkles (age rings).*

22

made his home with us when on leave. The market had added the option to become an auctioneer and so I was fortunate that if the war lasted another two years (and it seemed never ending at that time), I would have the opportunity to sample both worlds.

Accordingly, after presenting myself, without success, at Crewe Market Office for white-collar work, I left school and qualified as a farm labourer for Mr Watson, at Sunny Bank Farm, Rope, who also happened to have a very pretty daughter named Joan!! The present - day owner of Sunny Bank Farm is Mr David Dobson. My Father was 'frustrated', to put it mildly, at such a waste of a grammar school education! However, knowing of my ambitions, he used his influence as a regular customer at the Earl of Crewe public house which was

*'Progress' — the hose pipe replaces the bucket.*

tenanted, at that time, by the Mayor of the town, Mr Harry Bricker, who in turn used his connection with Mr Ernest Wright, the Managing Director of Messrs Henry Manley & Sons Ltd..

The old adage 'It's who you know not what you know' came to relevance and on the following Monday I was escorted by Mr Harry to Mr Ernest, who after a brief interview wished to meet my Father. The following Monday, Father had to take me again to the Gresty Road office where he was informed that I had the opportunity to join the staff, and that Henry Manley & Sons Ltd. no longer charged a fee for articled pupils but paid a pocket wage, (which was just as well, because my Father had no money to pay in any case). The wage was to be ten shillings per week and I was to start work at the Whitchurch

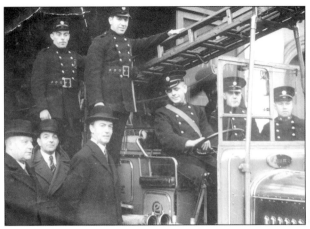

*Harry Bricker (extreme left), former Mayor of Crewe Borough, inspecting the new fire engine.*

office the following Monday; and would Father arrange for me to be kitted out with two slops and a pair of wellingtons?

Out of the pocket wage had to be paid the train fare from Crewe to Whitchurch; so even with a concessionary rail allowance I was in debt from the beginning!

Day one for me at Whitchurch was the Monday market and I was posted to the calf section where I was to register the names and addresses of the vendors and I always remember the first one was Mr Alby Cliffe, Red Lion Farm, Sound – others were more difficult to spell from verbal pronunciations, eg. Broughall (Broffle), Cholmondeley (Chumley). The next two years were spent as an office junior doing all the mundane jobs that such a position entails. This included sheet-running, rostrum to office, droving; and another trip to the market on the alternate Fridays. Frank Lloyd & Sons, of Wrexham, had the franchise with Manley's on the alternate weeks.

Instructions from Mr Robert Manley were to count the stock numbers forward on 'their week'. Mr Robert was the sole survivor of the family but still showed a keen interest at nearly ninety years of age; and I recall his delight when I reported ... 'One cow Sir!' Manley's week had seen a thriving market in all sections with prominent local exhibitors, the Dodd Brothers and Ted Arthen, of Malpas; Robin Arden (in short pants); Arthur Bradshaw, Charlie Harding and Andrew Moreton. Distant buyers in attendance included the Brunts, from Leek, and Tom Campbell, from Cheadle, in Staffordshire.

24

*Whitchurch Smithfield, 1893.*

The Monday Market had been converted to a Grading Day in 1940 when the Ministry of Food were paymasters and all stock was graded to a set standard by a Butcher Grader and a Farmer Grader, with Ministry Graders acting as policemen. This entailed a lot of clerical work and form filling, with local names such as Jack Wynne and Dick Coppnell performing the role of Graders.

Poultry was still sold on the 'open market' and the two firms touted for entries. Here my task was to jump on the running board and shout "Bring them to Manley's, Sir?" The auctioneer was Robert Manley, and one of the buyers was Reenie, sister to Jack Eisenberg, The Gables, Nantwich. Mr Robert's extra reward for diligence to us lads – Dennis Earnshaw, Horace Stokes, Stuart Lee, Cyril Downward and myself – was to promise to take us hunting when the war was over.

*Whitchurch Smithfield on Market Day, 1939.*

*Whitchurch Fatstock Champion, 1950. Pictured, l-r, W.Bradbury, Butcher; Cyril Downward; the winner Charlie Weaver, Burley Dam; W.Stoker, Evison Butchers, Watergate Street, Whitchurch; F.Darlington, retired farmer, Ash, Whitchurch.*

Livestock hauliers at Whitchurch in those days included Mrs Grocott, a widow who was always dressed immaculately in breeches and stockings, and whose family continues in the haulage business to this day, under the banner of 'GroContinental'. Jack Purcell and Brian Kynaston were also in regular attendance.

Whitchurch Cattle Market, built by the local council and opened in 1875, served the town well in attracting farmers from North Shropshire and South Cheshire. It was demolished in 1975 to make way for the Kwiksave and Iceland supermarkets.

And so the groundwork was completed by assisting at farm sales, furniture sales, valuations and so on. In 1944, I joined the 'Royal Navy' for two and half years – which would need another book; suffice it to say that I was only in the navy for a fortnight when I was convinced that my future was not as a sailor but as an auctioneer.

**1947** – Demobilised and back to Henry Manley & Sons Ltd. along with Peter Wilson, Bill Bailey, Eric Lewis, Brian Robson, Cyril Downward, Tom Craven, Harold Wood and Les Passant. All discharged to join the wartime staff which had

*The Sales Ring, at Crewe, designed to accommodate 1,000 people.*

consisted of part-time farmers, others over military age and such colleagues who had failed the medical examination.

However, this sudden influx of staff led to a surplus of manpower and by the end of that year only one of the ex-service men remained, namely Les Passant. All the others had found positions with other firms.

In response to the post-war improvement in livestock breeding, together with the anticipated decontrol of the war time livestock marketing restrictions and regulations, it is to the credit of the directors of Henry Manley & Sons Ltd. that they had the foresight to make a substantial financial investment in the redevelopment of Crewe Cattle Market. This was firstly in the Barker Street Market, which was purpose-built to accommodate Pedigree Cattle Sales; then secondly in the Middle Market, which was specially designed to accommodate Pedigree Small Stock sales and the weekly Calf Sale which attracted entries in excess of one thousand head when the calving season was at its peak. The total cost of the redevelopment amounted to £100,000.

Norman Clare by this time had returned, in 1951, from the Royal Navy to occupy the calf rostrum. Geoff Moss was joined by Brian Robson in the Pedigree department in 1954 when Brian recommenced his career, and became a first class pedigree livestock auctioneer who was held in very high regard by the North West Friesian Society members. Gerald Elson, who was born and bred in Crewe, joined the firm

*Described as the 'finest in the country', Henry Manley & Sons' Attested Cattle Market, Crewe, was formally opened by the Earl of Shrewsbury, in January 1951. In the picture here are Stan Croft (white smock), Frank Young (extreme right), with Norman Abberley, the Secretary; Colton Latham, on the rostrum; Wesley Emberton, and Tom Consterdine (Mayor).*

27

*A market 'without rival' in England. The main entrance to Manley's new Livestock Emporium – now demolished, after just 50 years, for housing development.*

when he left school and eventually became the Company Secretary.

A very able stockman by the name of Tom Fowler was appointed as Market Foreman, in charge of the new premises. His dedicated service over the next thirty years was an outstanding contribution to the firm. Noted for his care and attention to the pedigree livestock, which arrived at Crewe from far and wide, at all hours of day and night, Tom was held in the highest regard amongst pedigree livestock breeders throughout Great Britain.

---

*The Farmer & Stock Breeder:*

# Crewe Shorthorns' New Roof

For the first time the Crewe Association of Shorthorn Breeders held their annual spring show and sale in the modern surroundings of Messrs. Henry Manley and Sons' recently completed new market premises. It was described in our report of the opening ceremony as a market without rival in England.

The sale was conducted by Messrs. Thornborrow and Co., acting in conjunction with the resident auctioneers.

At the show a heifer, Grenway Airdie Duchess 44th, from Mr. H.E.Towers won the female champhionship, with Mr.W.Cowx's cow standing reserve. Messrs.A.and B.Hindley brought out the best bull, the runner-up being Mr. J.Evan Morris' Jevan Lord Darlington 24th.

---

*The new market buildings – a view from one of the loading docks.*

*The Earl of Shrewsbury (right) with (l-r) Sir John Barlow, Col. A.Heywood, Ernest Wright.*

*Some of the guests who attended the opening luncheon, assemble outside the main entrance to the new market.*

*T.H.Jefferson, Auctioneer, and Mr Ernest Wright, Chairman, take the rostrum for the first time.*

# CHAPTER FOUR
## Beeston Castle Smithfield

Livestock sales commenced at Beeston Castle Market in about 1872 and were held by a man named Booth Hewitt, of The Rookery, Alpraham. Booth Hewitt is entered in the Parish Records as having married Georgina Hale Fisher, the daughter of William Hale Fisher who is described on the Marriage Certificate as a 'Gentleman'. The marriage took place at Chester Cathedral on 18th April, 1876.

The market was located in a building on the opposite side of the Beeston Castle Hotel to the present site and some evidence

**BEESTON**

CATTLE SALE - Beeston Castle Station Cattle Sale was held on Monday last, for stock etc by Mr Booth Hewitt who sold 69 beasts, nearly 400 sheep, pigs and calves being the property of farmers, the Earl of Haddington, Sir P.Egerton, G.Barbour Esq., JP, J.Higson Esq., JP, and others; there was a capital sale which was attended by buyers from Manchester, Liverpool, Runcorn, Hadfield, Frodsham, Widnes, Over, Winsford, Sandbach, Chester Birkenhead, Tarporley, Tatten-hall, Kingsley, Warrington, Wakefield, Northwich, Nantwich, Crewe, Middle-wich, Walsall, the Potteries etc.

was still in situ when I first became employed at Beeston in 1947. There were stalls and limited penning for small stock. Store pigs for instance were sold in the horse drawn shandries and delivered free of charge.

Booth Hewitt had developed a string of livestock sales adjoining railway stations at Malpas, Tattenhall Road, Calveley and Worleston, but time proved that the only centre which warranted investment was Beeston, which possessed one major advantage over all the others. Namely a clause in the initial agreement between Lord Tollemache, owner of the Peckforton Estate, and the Railway Company which committed them to stop all trains at Beeston! It also had the benefit of Crewe junction and the London – Holyhead main line, together with a coaching house at the Beeston Castle Hotel, occupied in those days by the Williamson family.

**ALDERSEY ARMS - TATTENHALL ROAD STATION CATTLE MART.**

MR. BOOTH HEWITT begs respectfully to announce that at the request of Mr. Jones and a large number of Farmers and others, he will hold the FORTNIGHTLY CATTLE SALES at the above Mart, commencing on Wednesday June 22nd, 1881. Parties will oblige by making their entries early, so that the same may be advertised in next week's papers.
N.B. - The Sales will be carried out on the principle of Cash Settlements on the day of Sales, and owners can receive the money immediately their Stock is sold.
Alpraham, Tarporley

*An early photograph of Beeston.*

Malpas was to survive in a much smaller way for another one hundred years under Frank Lloyd's, of Wrexham, who eventually became Jones & Son, and later Jones Peckover. From those early beginnings both the Hewitts and the Williamsons became prominent farming families in the county. It is interesting to appreciate the courtesy and good grammar in the following extract from the Chester Chronicle, December 1877, which indicates to some extent the character of the founder of Beeston Market:

Mr Booth Hewitt Auctioneer takes this opportunity of thanking his agricultural friends and the public generally for the liberal support given him for the last six years during which time he has held these sales at the above cattle market and trusts by strict attention and prompt settlements to still merit their kind patronage. We can assure them that his duty will be to further their interests and give satisfaction to both buyer and seller. The first sale in the New Year will be held

MALPAS AUCTION - The ususal fortnightly cattle auction took place at Malpas Station on Tuesday last, when Mr. Booth Hewitt had a large and brisk sale for the stock present. There were ten cart-loads and nine pens of pigs, and a few pens of sheep, and over 30 fat and store cows, besides a few horses and colts. The pigs and fat stock were keenly competed for and realised high prices, one cow fetching £27, another £25, and other large sums.

31

on Monday, January 14th, 1878, and sales will take place every alternate Monday until further notice. Mr Hewit respectfully solicits from his supporters the favour of early entries, when no expense and trouble will be spared to give each sale a proper and wide spread of publicity.

It is also evident from the archives, and judging by the number of instructions he received to conduct dispersal sales and tenant right valuations, that he was a capable valuer and popular throughout the area. Just a few are listed here:

| Date | Farm | Client |
|------|------|--------|
| 1881 | Greaves Farm, Tattenhall | Mr John Skelland |
| 8th August 1882 | Bank Farm, Carden, Malpas | Mr Wm Blake |
| 4th October 1882 | Douse Green, Cholmondeley | Mr Edward Hulme |
| | Rectory Farm, Delamere | Mr Roger Sheen |
| 6th March 1883 | Crewe Corporation Sewage Farm | Mr Jackson, Chairman of Crewe Corporation Farm Committee |
| 27th March 1884 | Gosland Green, Bunbury | Mr I Teacom Vernon |

To digress for a moment from dates and statistics and the reasons for the development of the auction system in livestock exchange; it is, to my thoughts, a very great credit to all those involved in the markets (drovers, hauliers, cattle dealers, buyers, sellers and Auction staff) that the instances have been extremely rare when an animal, whatever its value, has not reached its rightful destination. This is particularly so in the concept of present-day society, when so many elements respect neither person nor property.

Booth Hewitt died on March 1st, 1896, aged 54, having lost his wife Georgina six years earlier. He had issue of four sons and two daughters. Three of the sons I remember, in particular Richard who still remained at the family home,

On Thursday and Friday next, day, March Twenty-seventh and Twenty-eighth.

Important Sale at Gosland Green Farm, Bunbury, One mile from Calveley Station.

(Mr I.Teacom Vernon) under a Bill of Sale BY MR. BOOTH HEWITT, on Thursday and Friday next, March 27th and 28th, 1884 - 24 useful dairy cows and heifers, 15 of which will have calves at foot; 10 grand yearling calves and one bull, six in-pig sows, 45 store pigs, 30 couple fowls, five horses and colts, 150 measures black oats, 20 measures magnum potatoes, together with the whole of the implements of husbandry, neat lot of dairy vessels, very excellent and valuable HOUSEHOLD FURNITURE &c, &c.

Full particulars in Catalogues.

1st. day live stock, produce, implements, dairy vessels, and kitchen requisites, &c.

2nd. day household and bedroom furniture, &c.

Lunch first day by ticket at 11 o'clock.

Sale at 12 prompt.

Alpraham, Tarporley.

The Rookery, Alpraham, and who was employed by the new principal of the firm, Mr Joseph Wright. Richard had been too young to succeed his father. The sole survivor of the Hewitt family is Mr Ted Hewitt, ex-Cheshire Yeomanry,

who resides in Eaton as a retired gentleman and has been so helpful in providing material for this book.

Mr Joseph Wright had been engaged in the Hewitt enterprise for some years in a clerical capacity and, it would appear, was obliged to become an auctioneer at comparatively short notice. As the following chapter will reveal he was able to build on the excellent foundations provided by Booth Hewitt. Much of his success in the ensuing years was based on a strong religious faith in the Methodist Creed, and his involvement in the church created excellent connections in the farming communities throughout the county. He was to be ably supported both in his endeavours at his growing success at Beeston, and in his legacy of religion, by his two sons, Harold and Joseph (young Joe). Joseph Willet Wright formed a partnership with his two sons, Harold and Joseph, in the early 1920's.

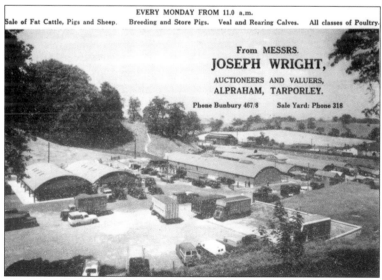

EVERY MONDAY FROM 11.0 a.m.

Sale of Fat Cattle, Pigs and Sheep. Breeding and Store Pigs. Veal and Rearing Calves. All classes of Poultry.

From MESSRS.
**JOSEPH WRIGHT,**
AUCTIONEERS AND VALUERS,
ALPRAHAM, TARPORLEY.

Phone Bunbury 467/8      Sale Yard: Phone 318

*Beeston Castle Smithfield, 1957.*

33

*Joe Cowap.*

Between the wars many of the 'station markets' closed and those that survived were saved by the Second World War, when Ministries prolonged their usage as collecting centres for the grading of livestock. Beeston established itself as the sole country market for dairy cattle, store cattle and calves, as well as a grading centre. That Beeston survived and thrived was due in no small part to its figurehead, whose connections were invaluable. His handshake to all his customers at the market gate was a byword, and accordingly he was recognised as both an auctioneer and a gentleman.

The rostrum duties were performed primarily by son Harold, assisted by Richard Hewitt. Young Joe was responsible for cashier's duties and the auctioneer's clerks included Mr Billy Hewitt, who farmed with his brother at Hill Farm, Rushton. The droving staff were recruited on a part-time basis from the many smallholders in the area looking for supplementary income. The basis of this teamwork was more than helpful in so far as it was able to thread its way through the entire fabric of country life, although Beeston could not at that time provide the commercial advantages of the town centre markets of Crewe and Chester.

The second generation had now produced a third when both Harold Wright and Alan Wright were born in the 1920's and were weaned into mar-

CHRISTMAS CATTLE SALE AT BEESTON

The annual sale at this Mart was held on Monday under circumstances favourable alike to buyer and seller. As on previous occasions of this kind, the company was very numerous, between 600 and 700 people being in the yard at one time. The whole of these were not of course connected with the legitimate business on hand, viz., buying and selling cattle. The number, however, in this respect was very considerable, the buyers being in excess of any former occasion, and such being the case a sharp competition resulted, especially animals having the appearance of Christmas stock. For these, Mr.Booth Hewitt, the auctioneer, offered prizes as follows: £2 2s for the best heifer under three years old (Mr. Wright being the winner). This animal was sold for £25. Mr. Johnson, of Bulkeley Hall, near Malpas, took the prize of £1 1s for the best fat bull, which realized £30. His animal was closely followed by Mr Williamson's, of the Hotel. £1 1s was given for the best fat bullock. The competition in this class was not numerous, and Mr. Wright carried away the prize. £1 1s, given to the owner of the best fat beast realizing the highest price and which did not win a prize, was secured by Mr. Williamson by his bull, which made £29 15s. The prizes for the sheep and pigs went to Messrs Wright and Gregory respectively, the prizes being for four sheep £3 10s 6d each, and four pigs £7 8s each. Half a guinea was given to the owner of the best fat calf, which sold for £5 9s., Mr. Perry, of Spurstow, being awarded this prize. In addition the auctioneer gave to the butchers and farmers a lunch which was partaken by about 500. There were sold during the day about 125 head of horned stock, 500 pigs, 150 sheep and a few calves. The manner is which the stock was disposed of and dispersed was creditable alike to the auctioneer and his assistants. A word of praise is due to Mrs.Williamson for the manner in which the catering for such a number of persons was done.

34

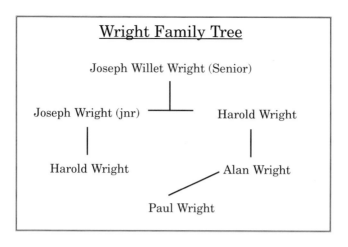

# Wright Family Tree

Joseph Willet Wright (Senior)

Joseph Wright (jnr) — — Harold Wright

Harold Wright — Alan Wright

Paul Wright

ket service, to play their part with other family members who included George Charlesworth (Harold's uncle) and the whole operation was conducted from the family home – The Elms, at Alpraham. During the Second World War, Harold and Alan were both called to the colours and exactly how the business survived I often wonder, but it was no doubt a major factor that Joseph Wright was appointed, by the government of the day, County Chairman of Auctioneers and was, therefore, responsible for the payment to farmers for all the fat stock presented through all the livestock centres in the county, including

*Xmas 1963 – Mr Copeland, right, the Bailiff to Lord Rocksavage, of Cholmondeley, and Miss Copeland. Also pictured are: Mr J.A.Wright, John Vernon, Butcher, Broxton; Mr F.Burrows, Butcher, Bunbury; George Hill, Butcher, Malpas.*

*These photographs and the following extract are courtesy of Cheshire Life, published October, 1979: "...Beeston livestock market where generations of Cheshire's stockmen have worn smooth the benches at the ringside and where the air is thick with pipe smoke and speculation. This is a job for professionals; the visitor stands out as noticeably as a daffodil in a cow pat. One old hand commented dryly that 'visitors are the only ones who look where they walk'."*

*The photographs include: (clockwise) – Sam Barnes (Burw ardsley), Bob Moss, Onnerley, Woore; Harold Barnes, Manchester; Trevor Poskitt, Doncaster; Richard Whitehead, Brereton; Morrel Glover, Shrewsbury; Ray Ellwood, Nantwich; Ron Tomkinson, Leighton; Billy Swindells, Stockport; Ted Arthan, Malpas.*

Crewe and Chester, much to the surprise of the firms operating those big centres at that time.

A setback was to occur in 1936, when son Harold (Alan's father) died from pneumonia, a condition which claimed so many lives at that time and, from a year or two afterwards, so few. The firm had lost its primary salesman who, like his father, had established himself as an auctioneer of high repute. Again the next Joseph Wright (young Joe) was to move from the office to the rostrum 'overnight', and the firm continued as a father and son partnership until Joseph Wright Snr. died in 1942.

A contribution is timely at this point from Mr George Ford, who has also helped me a lot in my research. George, who was employed at Chester Market by Leonard Wright, recalls this desperate moment when Joseph Wright, Beeston, rang Leonard Wright, Chester, for help in Beeston rostrum through his sad loss. George was sent along with Mr Joseph Cowap, of Fishers Green, Utkinton, who, by coincidence, was brother-in-law to the deceased, and worked as a part-time auctioneer at Chester. Alan Wright, therefore, inherited 'Auctioneer's Blood' from both parents!

It is also timely to mention the unusual coincidence of the surname Wright. Ernest Wright was the managing director of Henry Manley's, of Crewe; Joseph Wright was the family head at Beeston, Leonard Wright was the head of the Chester Market; and Stanley Wright was the principal of Mainwaring & Stafford, at Warrington Auction. Yet not one of them was related!

*A big attraction at the 1957 Nantwich Festival – milking cattle on the Civic Hall car park.*

# CHAPTER FIVE
## Chester Cattle Market

For seven centuries Chester has been a centre for livestock marketing where cattle fairs were held originally. Then for four centuries there was a beast market, right in the middle of the city. The first auction market was held at the Ermine Cattle Mart in the 1870's and was conducted by auctioneers named Pickering Sons & Woodfin, on the site occupied today by the Ermine public house, on Hoole Road. Great excitement and confusion were created in the area when cattle were driven to market from farms in the local areas; or unloaded from the Lightfoot Street pens having arrived by rail from the more outlying districts.

Subsequently, the firm became Pickering & Nightingale and eventually only Mr Nightingale survived which led to the eventual demise of the Ermine Market. This was brought about, no doubt, by the decision of the Chester City Council to take an interest in the increasing popularity of the livestock auction marketing system and the building of a new Cattle Market in 1884, between George Street and Gorse Stacks – so called from its use as a site for the stacking of gorse for fuel – and also the site where Seddons had a salt warehouse.

This would obviously increase the number of livestock in the area on Market Days. I well remember hearing of many heart-stopping occasions when cattle arriving over Cow Lane

On Tuesday, December 14th, 1880, GRAND CHRISTMAS SALE and SHOW of Fat Stock, at the ERMINE CATTLE MART., CHESTER. PICKERING SONS & WOODFIN, will hold their annual SALE and SHOW of Fat CATTLE, SHEEP, PIGS and CALVES on Tuesday December 14, 1880.
The present entries include—
95 Grand fat Bullocks, Cows and Heifers
8 Splendid fat Bulls (heavy weights)
120 Ripe fat Sheep
98 Prime fat Bacon and Proket Pigs
15 Ditto Calves
The following PRIZES will be awarded by two competent Judges before the sale commences.
£3 for the best fat Bullock, any age, the winner to give the purchaser £1.
£3 for the best fat Cow, any age, the winner to give the purchaser £1.
£3 for the best fat Heifer, any age, the winner to give the purchaser £1.
£3 for the best fat Bull, any age, the winner to give the purchaser £1.
£2 for the best pen of not less than five fat Sheep, the winner to give the purchaser 10s.
£2 for the best pen of not less than three fat Pigs, the winner to give the purchaser 10s.
£3 for the best five Beasts in the sale yard, the property of one person.
£1 for the best fat Calf.
All stock entered for competition must have been in the owner's possession not less than two months prior to sale, and must be bona fide sold for slaughter.
Further entries respectfully solicited.
Settlement with owners immediately after sale.
Sale to commence not later than 10 o'clock.

Bridge invaded local shops and business premises, which was simply accepted as part of life. Such situations today would provide Chester Courts with enough cases for compensation for a long time to come.

The New Market was in two sections, the Smithfield and the Agricultural Hall. The former was let to Messrs Cunnagh & Roberts, and the latter to Sydney R. Fearnall. Thus, once again, as in the Crewe development, three markets were competing for the business of auctioning livestock.

The Ermine Market eventually closed leaving the two firms – both tenants to the council – competing for business. This situation continued for many years until Roberts died, Cunnagh retired and Sydney Fearnall relinquished the Agricultural Hall. Leonard Wright who was a farmer's son and whose brother farmed at Church House, Alvanley, had started work in the Smithfield in 1908. He became a member of the Auctioneers Institute in 1919 and successfully tendered for both markets. So, as in Crewe at the beginning of the century, three markets became one at Chester under the new heading Leonard Wright & Company, who opened their first offices in Union Buildings, Newgate Street. In an astute move, Leonard invited Leigh Sadler to join him. Leigh had joined Sydney Fearnall, from Kings School, in 1907, and was a partner with him at the time. He also attracted Les Foster and Frank Tranter to join him as junior partners, with Lou Davies as secretary.

In addition to Chester, Leonard Wright conducted weekly sales at Hooton and the New Inn, Greasby, which had been founded as branches to the Ermine Market. He also acted as Secretary, through Les Foster, to Frodsham Farmers Auction Co. which held sales behind the Bears Paw pub, in the High Street. The reader will note that markets were sited either by the railway station or the pub, ideally adjacent to both. The pubs remain, but, thanks to Dr Beeching, the stations have gone.

39

*Opening of the New Attested Market at Gorse Stacks, in 1955, by Leonard Wright (white smock) and including Frank Tranter, Claude Chrimes, Mayor of Chester, and Mr Greenwood, Chester City Surveyor. In the ring is Mr Edge, Tattenhall.*

*Leonard Wright in the new cattle pens.*

40

Chester Market developed successfully over the next thirty years competing with Crewe as to which could lay claim to be the largest centre for the sale of commercial stock, particularly Dairy Cattle and Cull Cows (Barrens).

It attracted cattle dealers country-wide, with one outstanding name, Bobby Richards, from Oswestry, who would show over one hundred milk cows on a Thursday and clear the lot to farmers and the trade through the sale ring. An indelible memory of mine from Leonard Wright – Quote: 'Look after the seller. The buyer will look after himself.'

**LEONARD WRIGHT & CO.**
Auctioneers, Valuers, Land & Estate Agents
SEDAN HOUSE, GORSE STACKS, CHESTER
CHESTER SMITHFIELD
SALES BY AUCTION EVERY TUESDAY of
FAT CATTLE, PIGS AND SHEEP
REARING AND VEAL CALVES
ALL CLASSES OF STORE POULTRY

EVERY THURSDAY
BARREN & TURNOFF COWS; also FAT BULLS
DAIRY COWS AND HEIFERS
STORE CATTLE
Sales commence each day at 11.30am
2,500 HEAD OF STOCK SOLD WEEKLY
*THE CHRONICLE AUGUST 17, 1963*

*David Fisher selling at Chester in the days when Cull Cows were exported. Now, with half the world starving, how much longer will we continue to burn them?*

# CHAPTER SIX
## The Post War Years - A New Beginning

With the war over, young men returned to their roots still with the aspirations of youth, and Joseph Wright was also looking to the future in establishing the family firm with his expanding ambitions.

'Invest in People' is a modern cliché, but Joseph Wright did just that in 1947. He attracted Tommy Henderson, from Newcastle-under-Lyme, in Staffordshire, and housed him in the wooden offices at The Elms, Alpraham, which had been built to accommodate the staff required for his position as County Chairman during the War years.

Here he was to work alongside those devoted servants who had been retained over the war period. The Ministry staff were led by Frank Hall (ex-1914-18) who hated Germany with good reason, having lost part of his hip in the trenches and a son (RAF 1939-1945); also Neville Turner, who was accommodated by the Johnson family at the Travellers Rest, at Alpraham, returning to his home and that of the family firm of auctioneers, in Macclesfield, at weekends.

One of many memories when waiting with Neville at the bus stop at Alpraham was meeting the Hunt. The Hunt was blocking the main road and the bus was late. Turner confronted the Master (unheard of in 1948) with the words... 'Move you and your bloody hounds out of it. I've got a connection to catch at Crewe – it's buggers like you who will turn this country Communist!' The beginning of anti-blood sports maybe!

Tommy Henderson proved to be an excellent servant and Joe made sure that he wasn't tempted back to Staffordshire by buying him a house in Tarporley. He remained a valuable asset to the firm for the rest of his life. Further increases in staff followed to service new offices at Northwich, Winsford and Nantwich, together with a shrewd purchase, from Frank Lloyd's, of a rundown office and a market franchise at Whitchurch.

These vacancies, plus those required for a growing business at Beeston, were filled by poaching ex-Henry Manley & Sons Ltd. staff in Peter Wilson, Brian Robson, Harold Wood and yours truly. Harold and Alan Wright returned from the Armed Forces at the same time and the first team had been formed.

My interview had taken place at The Elms on a Sunday morning in September 1947 and as there was no Sunday bus service, I persuaded a cousin with a car to provide transport. After a thorough inquisition, Mr Wright sat back and suddenly exclaimed ... 'I understand you like a drink!'

I realised from his well known religion that he would be a tee-totaller  and I replied with the awful, honest truth ...

'Yes Sir!'

'Well I'll tell you one thing.  If I ever find you have been drinking in my time, you won't get a month's notice or a week, you'll be up that road straight away!  Go home and tell your Mother you're on trial for a month.'

During the next five years I developed a very deep respect for my principal and, in my mind, was rewarded before his death in 1952 – he had offered to buy me a home near to my work, which demonstrated his appreciation of my efforts. I also remained teetotal during working hours for the rest of my life.

Amongst many recollections of that period, a simple example of his role of 'the boss' was when I arrived ten minutes late to be remonstrated on the matter; to which I gave one of my rare retorts, 'It's only ten minutes Sir!'. He replied by pointing to an ex-army truck that was waiting for me with six men ready to go to a farm sale.

'Six tens are sixty, that's an hour's pay to me!'

'But Charlie hasn't come yet – we can't go without him?'

'We'll count him dead, and then we'll have to do without him.  On your way!'

On the very human side, one Saturday morning, I asked ... 'Could I have next Saturday off Sir?'

'Why?' ... came the reply.

'I'm getting married,' I said.

*Tommy Henderson 'at work' with George Charlesworth.*

43

*Early days when this part of Wrenbury provided the surrounding areas with a cattle market, a pub (The Salamanca), a bank and a railway station, of which only the latter remains in operation.*

'You can't afford to get married,' said Mr Wright.

'Quite right, Sir,' I replied, and silence followed.

The following Tuesday at Wrenbury Auction, Mr Wright approached me and said...

'Brian, I'd like a word about your marriage next Saturday.'

'Yes Sir?' I replied.

'I've given you a rise in salary from £4 to £5 per week.'

'Thank you, Sir!' I said.

'Oh, and here's a present,' whereby he counted £25 out in £1 notes on the wall of Wrenbury Auction Office.

When relating this story to one of the present staff, he remarked, 'Was that all?' To which I replied, 'Multiply your wages by six and tell me if you still think, was that all?'.

Wrenbury Market was the first auction market in Cheshire built by Henry Manley, in 1860. It operated successfully until some time after the First World War when it became Wrenbury Farmers' Auction Company.

This transition coincided with the move of Ernest Wright from Frank Lloyd & Co. to Henry Manley & Sons Ltd. when local farmers suspected, probably with good reason, that he was encouraging the sale of livestock to Crewe! Gordon Cooke was put in charge at Wrenbury and the market was eventually acquired by Joseph Wright. It came back into its own during the Second World War and the post - war years of Ministry control, when it became the collection centre with the largest throughput in the county.

The graders were George Thomasson, of Frith Hall, and Walter Hockenhull, the local butcher, from Aston. The man virtually in charge was Hughie Williams, who controlled the situation by entering the number of animals required for market capacity and local traders and farmers made up any shortfall. He was also well informed on movements within the Ministry, and I soon learned that if I had a call to arrive very early on a Tuesday morning then the super grader was to attend the market. But by the time he arrived, many animals had been graded, allocated and dispatched!

Hughie was a very popular man in the area and also well connected in racing circles. I had a personal regard for him through being a neighbour for three years and well recall an incident when his sheep strayed into my field, which was also full of sheep. Hughie arrived to say, 'Brian, I can soon sort mine out, they are all punched (Ministry earmarks),' only to be told, 'So are mine Mr Williams.'

'No problem,' he said, 'You take one and I'll take the next and so on,' and the situation was resolved. His popularity continues through 'Wick', his stepbrother on a neighbouring farm.

The market pub, The Salamanca, which is now closed, was kept latterly by Mr Wilf Speed. It was within its cloisters that I heard the definition of a 'grouper', a description given to Abler Thomasson by

*Tommy Henderson selling sheep in 'The Sheds' at Beeston in 1962.*

45

Vic Adams. The former asked the meaning of the word and Vic replied, 'You were born in the group (the manure end of a cow stall) and your mother never licked you!' All good bar-room banter.

After several failed attempts to hold periodic sales, Wrenbury Market was sold as a caravan site.

Joseph Wright's son, Harold, was moved to Whitchurch, to take charge there and was joined by Cyril Downward. Together they were to expand the business into North Shropshire. Peter Wilson, who had many farming and veterinary connections, took a lot more business from the established firms in South Cheshire. Alan Wright remained with his uncle at the hub of the business whilst Tommy Henderson, or T.D.H. as he was affectionately known, undertook the bulk of the professional work, which grew rapidly during that period. Brian Robson and I

*Beeston Xmas Fatstock 1955 – left to right: Miss Leech (Mrs Boughey), Arthur Leech (Peckforton Hall), Alan Wright, Vic Millward (Butcher), Tarporley, Harry Garner (Butcher), Cuddington, John Wood, Norbury, YFC Steward.*

*Beeston Xmas Fatstock Champion 1960, including Mr Nield, Tattenhall, Mr Moss, Weaverham, Alf Wilding, Winsford, Mr Barrett, Wrenbury.*

filled the gaps and all of us would be at Beeston on a Friday to undertake everything that needed doing to provide the best possible service.

Peter Wilson married Joan Cook who worked in the Alpraham office and was the daughter of Gordon Cook who had been the firm's representative at Wrenbury Auction in the 1930's. Alan Wright married Betty Moors who also worked in the offices and was daughter to a prominent butcher from Over, Winsford.

Butchers were of great value in their early support of the auction system and helped to improve the vital social link between town and country, developing the livestock market, not merely as the medium

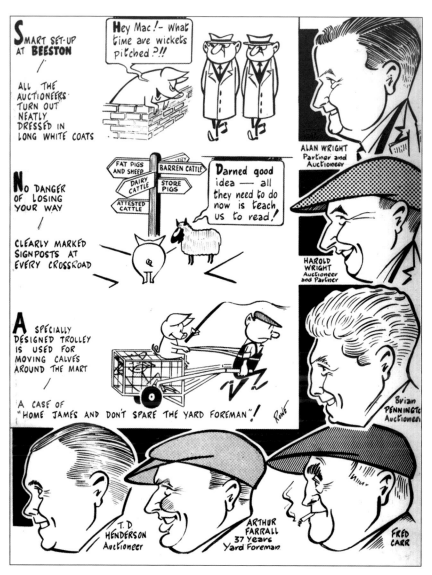

*Farmers Guardian cartoon in the early 1950's.*

for converting cattle into cash, but also to create a social connection between farmers, corn and implement merchants etc, to say nothing of an up-date in 'gossip' appending to various localities. Many 'local butchers' had their own slaughter-houses. Every big town, or city, had its own abattoir and wholesale meat market, which generated keen competition in the auction ring.

Meat Inspection was in its early stages of application, the pole axe preceded the captive bolt pistol, and the deal that was done outside the sale ring was sealed by a hand shake or slap, accompanied with a phrase of trust for payment, 'Here's my hand and here's my heart.'

The licensing of slaughter-houses and the outbreak of war, in 1939, brought an end to many of these outlets when the Ministry of Food controlled supplies of all meat. Grading systems were introduced for all classes of slaughter stock which were presented at local market centres, then weighed and graded by a panel consisting of a farmer, a butcher and a Ministry representative. Even calves were graded, other than those retained for rearing, and I recall the following price schedule:

| Category | Price |
| --- | --- |
| Reject | 3s 6d |
| BCT (Bull Calf Ten Shilling) | 10s 0d |
| Small Bobby | 18s 0d |
| Medium | 25s 0d |
| Large | 30s 0d |
| VC3 (Veal Calf 3rd Grade) | |
| eg 44 lbs @ 9d | 33s 0d |
| and so on to a maximum of about | £ 8 0s 0d |

*The new Poultry Shed nearing completion at Beeston, late 1950's, having been dismantled and moved from Wrenbury Market.*

48

A piece of poetry received at that time, written by the late Joseph Nicholas, the youngest son of the late Mr Ken Nicholas, of Acton Bridge, Nr Northwich, captures the relationship which prevailed between the Farmer and the Grader.

### 'A Plea to the Ministry Graders'

This is a plea to the Ministry Graders,
Please, be fair to all meat traders,
For when we farmers take our cattle to the mart,
Surely the Graders should play their part.
To give us a fair deal that's all we ask,
Surely that isn't too hard a task.
But "it's short on the shoulders", or "a shade too fat"
There's always something wrong with this or that,
"It's got no loin", or "It's got no arse",
Isn't this grading lark nowt but a farce.
And of course we know what's coming next,
Upon its haunches that little green x.
Then it's into the ring with that gradely look,
Which the butchers buy, to get passed on the hook.
Then it's off to the slaughterhouse to get those passes.
Those previously crossed cattle, in all their masses.
And it's not the butcher's fault, it's their job,
To try and make a few extra bob,
And the auctioneers too, do their bit,
To persuade the Graders the cattle are fit.
But sadly it's the Graders that have the last word,
And some of their decisions seem totally absurd,
So, if we dare lay our hands on them, I've got a hunch,
It's the Graders who'd be getting the punch!

Needless to say, for obvious reasons, it was never published in our 'Weekly Market News' bulletin. Although, it must be said, for most of the time we all got on very well. The Ministry Grader was always in a difficult situation!

As in all matters which involve money and human nature, some markets were more generous with their standards than others and some farmers and farmer/dealers were blessed with the ability to influence the graders' decisions and to 'play the market'. Some markets, including Crewe, Beeston and Chester, therefore exploited the opportunity to hold sales 'on the hoof', thus creating an option to the farmer to 'grade or sell'.

*Beeston from the Bank in the mid 1950's.*

Graders to my memory are listed below:

**Crewe** – Sam Henshall, Shavington; Mr Woodcock, Moat Farm, Wistaston; Harry Moss, Worleston.

**Beeston** – Bill Cowap, Tarporley; Harry Garner, Cuddington; Tommy Oulton, Ferney Lees; Frank Pleavin, Kelsall; Arthur Walley, Winterford, Eaton; Alf Barker, Rushton; Frank Gleave, Middlewich.

**Chester** – Arthur Charmley, Chester; Philip Oakden, Wirral; Harold Hanley, Vicars Cross.

All were kept in order in those days by the 'Men from the Ministry' including, Ron Ravenscroft, George Excel, Mr Goulding, Alan Brighton, Philip Henshaw and Frank Mylchreest, amongst others.

In 1954, when the government announced decontrol, all classes of stock previously bought and distributed by the Ministry, were to find their price on the open market, with the retention of some subsidies which had been introduced during the war years. A lot of the slaughterhouses never re-opened. Many others succumbed in the ensuing years to the requirements of the civil service, and so a lot of butchers departed from the ringside.

The largest meeting of livestock auctioneers ever to take place in the North West was convened by the Ministry of Agriculture, Fisheries & Food at the Station Hotel, Preston, in Lancashire, where a government spokesman, with very inaudible deliveries, outlined the future situation. At the end of the meeting the silence was broken from the rear of the hall with a vote of thanks from the loudest voice I have ever heard. It was that of Leonard Wright, of Chester.

Beeston Market was originally a group of galvanised iron sheds, a

50

*The first store cattle ring almost completed for the first sale in 1957 – Brian Pennington and Harold Wright in the rostrum. Others in the picture include Fred Holland Senior, Tiverton, Frank Jones, Spurstow, T.G. Ford, Eardswick Hall, with son Geoff and Brian Hancock (with hair).*

small office, and a café of similar construction, approached from the A49 through a clump of trees with its boundary denoted by a paling fence at the entrance. It has grown to its present size by courtesy of extensive sand quarrying into the hill – the only remaining original feature being the cottage at the entrance. It has been added to in an ad hoc manner, as it grew from its humble beginnings, by purchases from markets which were losing ground such as Wrenbury, Frodsham and Northwich. Whilst the present offices were formerly the President's Pavilion at the Royal Lancashire Agricultural Showground, at Wrea Green, Blackpool. Further developments in recent years include a purpose-built calf market and a Pedigree Sales Centre.

As Beeston became more popular, its restricted area at the bottom of a hillside with the entrance also serving as the exit, called for the early services of 'Blaster Bates' who detonated the clump of trees, which relieved some of the pressure of 'pouring a quart into a pint pot'! Queues were seen as far back as Beeston Towers (Wild Boar), controlled by the local policeman (who also issued pig licences) and any of us who were not on duty in a rostrum, or on a sales plank.

Young Joe was seeing the success of his efforts when yet another misfortune hit the firm, with his sudden premature death at the age of 56, on February 16th, 1952. He was interred in Tilstone Fearnall Churchyard, and his funeral was one of the largest the countryside

51

*Xmas Sheep Sale 1960. Includes, left to right: Ron Handley, Christleton; Fred Hodgson, Oxheys; Alf Barker, Rushton; Bill Garner, Cuddington; Mr Cowap, Tilstone Bank; Tom Ball, Eaton; Mr Burrows, Ellesmere Port; Mr Gosmore and Mr Nield, Tattenhall; Mr Stubbs, Crowton; Cyril Downward and Tom Henderson.*

*Fat Cattle Ring 1962 – Auctioneer, Alan Wright; Clerk, Noel Guest. Also includes: Mr Goulding (Grader) watching the scales to 'police' subsidy payments; Mr Peacock and Mr Latham, of Chorley; John Atherton, Weaverham; Harry Jones, Spurstow; Peter Holland, Davenham; John Lightfoot, Kingsley; John Fernyhough, Chester; Fred Rutter, Beeston; Mr Burrows, Bunbury; Mr Cowap, Tarporley; Buyer for Hindford Co-op; Fred Holland, Tiverton; Arthur Green, Kidsgrove; David Holland, Weaverham.*

had ever seen. Harold Wright, by succession, became head of the firm overnight and, in good family faith, formed a partnership with his cousin, Alan. The County Chairmanship was lost. Peter Wilson who had become popular in property sales formed his own business, and Brian Robson was tempted back to Henry Manley & Sons Ltd., at Crewe.

Fortunately, Harold and Alan had also inherited the family ambitions for progress. There were redundancies and re-ranking and Beeston, whilst still very much 'the small country market', was nevertheless the flagship of the firm JOSEPH WRIGHT.

*Harold and Alan Wright in 1962.*

*Covered areas were very limited in the old market.*

# CHAPTER SEVEN
## The Developing Years

Beeston had always been a Monday market and had introduced a Dairy Cattle Sale on alternate Fridays. These were increased to weekly sales and now the new young partners and staff were full of enthusiasm to build a market to rank with the big centres, particularly Crewe and Chester, which lay equidistant to the east and west. T.D.H. took the Dairy Section in the Upper Market, while Alan and I worked in the Lower Market, and one of the first steps was to introduce a Pedigree Friesian Sale which received only qualified support.

Immediately to my mind springs the occasion when acting as clerk to T.D.H. I was asked to obtain the reserve of the next beast to be sold from Mr E.S. Oswell, who at that time farmed at Woodford Hall, Winsford. The reply to the question was 'Two Thirty', an unheard of figure at Beeston! I looked at the animal for sale, a 'shelly' sort to my commercial mind. Thought for a moment, had another look and

*Early morning in Beeston, from the railway, showing offices adjacent to the cottage, and the cafe, by the Farmers Guardian caravan. The traffic master is Frank Hough, of Alpraham.*

decided Mr Oswell had not heard me properly and was telling me the time. I repeated the question, and had the same reply. After one more look I went to the toilet, and let Tommy ask for his own reserve. The beast made 230 guineas, to everyone's amazement apart from my own. Try as we may, Crewe had cornered the Pedigree Livestock Sector in the North West, and we were to enter later through the back door.

*Ted Oswell, Woodford Hall, and Arthur Leech, Peckforton Hall, exchange pleasantries with Arthur Moors, Butcher, of Over, Winsford.*

As well as Barren Cows, I was in charge of the Store Pig Section and decided that, in view of the heavy losses fatteners suffered through Swine Fever, I would introduce a special sale for pigs vaccinated against the disease. The date of the prize sale came and to my embarrassment there were no entries. Shortly afterwards Mr J.D. Pickering, of Marlston-cum-Lache, Nr Chester, instructed me to conduct a sale of vaccinated pigs on his premises. This was also a failure, and in words of some commiseration I recall his wisdom, 'Brian, we are just a little before our time.' How right he was, and twelve months later we started again.

> **Week 1.** I had one pen and a telephone call from a stranger called Richardson from Blackpool who instructed me to buy them on his behalf. He rang back later and was told I had not bought them as I considered them too dear!
>
> **Week 2.** Eight pens ... same man ... same instructions ... call later ... same reply, with the pigs at least £2 per head more than non-vaccinated.
>
> **Week 3.** Twelve pens ... same instructions ... same reply ... to hear Mr Richardson, who had passed no comment in the previous weeks say ... 'Young man, you are a fool! How the hell do you expect to get the scheme working if you can't make the price attractive? I'll come myself next week!' He sent his son Bill who bought all of the increased entry of twenty pens; and the family still sup-

ports the firm from the Fylde Coast, to this day. This was to be the start of Beeston becoming one of the biggest weekly Store Pig Sales in the UK with entries in excess of 2000 head; and attracting buyers from as far afield as Greater London.

There were more local buyers, such as Chris Allman, of Whitchurch; Bert Bleasdale, Ledsham; Fred Vernon and Jessie Ashworth, Swill Feeders from Failsworth, Nr Manchester; and Mr R. E. Hughes, from Telpyn, Ruthin; along with many prominent farmers who fed large numbers of pigs to consume whey, or as a second string to milk production, such as the Willis family, from Chester and Whitchurch; the Rogers family, from Wrexham; Tommy Hastings, from Rossett; and Mr Roland Astbury, Sandiway, Nr Northwich.

The success of the vaccinated scheme came to an end when the government of the day introduced a slaughter policy for the eradication of the disease. Accordingly, the sales ceased. However, with the connections that we had established we were called upon to conduct valuations on behalf of the Ministry over a very wide area, and eventually the disease was totally eradicated.

In addition, through the slaughter policies adopted for the eradication of other diseases, eg Aujesky's, T. B., Foot & Mouth, and B.S.E., we worked frequently with Ministry vets. The great majority were very co-operative and understanding. Local favourites with us all were Charlie Stewart, of Chester, and Bernard Brown, of Sandbach, who

*Store pigs at Beeston.*

56

*'Little & Large'. Early days of the Beeston Horse Sales, showing the author's youngest daughter, Jane, with the Shetland, and Doug Jennings, of Market Drayton, with the Shire.*

possessed the character and good sense to smooth over many difficult problems which naturally arise in compulsory purchase situations.

I recall one of the valuations at a smallholding in Lancashire, when a canny pig farmer described one of the pens as 'twenty-five in-pig gilts'. After a closer look I queried his description – they did not look pregnant to me. He replied that actually there were only twenty-four...the other was a boar! I was to learn 'quietly', later, that the boar had been introduced to the pen on the previous day!

An annual sale of Agricultural Implements and Machinery had been held in a field at Oakmere, near Northwich, for several years. When a substantial increase in the rent paid for the field was proposed, Alan Wright and I decided to relocate the sale to the newly-extended area, behind the Dairy Cattle Shed at Beeston, which had been recently acquired by the partners from the Peckforton Estate. This move proved to be a great success and the Machinery Sale became a monthly Market Fixture; although it never developed to quite the same scale as the Cambridge Machinery Sales. Slowly but surely through different people coming from different walks of life, from areas 'foreign' to Beeston at that time, all helped to spread the name – BEESTON!

There were names such as Morgan, from Doncaster, who had connections in the Sheffield Tool Trade, and Mr Johnston, a supplier of railway sleepers and timber, from Westhoughton, in Lancashire. Also many came from North Wales, including a character who when asked for his name replied 'Tom Jim'. This was regarded at the time as a rude and rather facetious answer. However, it transpired to be his adopted trading title, with which he even signed his cheques to avoid any possible confusion with others of a similar name. It was, of course, the renowned Mr Tom Jim Roberts, from Bryn-Banon Bach, Llanfor, Nr Bala.

The long-term survival of any regular sales fixture always depends on a dedicated band of loyal supporters. Traders such as Bob Coxen, of Chester, and Mick Mellor, of Crewe, who have supplied the sales with timber and steel in suitable lots for the farming community, year in year out, in all kinds of weather conditions. Similarly, in the Machinery Lines, L.Parry & Sons, from Chester, and Ted Bownes, of Winsford, were always in regular attendance, regardless of the prevailing economic climate.

At about the same time, I was approached by Dr. Ewing, of Weaverham, who asked if I was prepared to occupy the rostrum for horse and pony sales at premises in Warrington, which he would acquire. This was at a time when the demand for workhorses had become confined to the knacker yards and led to the demise of the once thriving horse sales at Crewe, Wrexham and Chester. I was in no position to contract out of my employment under Joseph Wright and with some regret told him so.

After a short time I realised the potential behind the doctor's thoughts in that the light horse and pony were becoming popular with the thriving middle classes through shows and gymkhanas. After discussing the matter with Harold and Alan Wright, I returned to the doctor for his blessing to

*A packed Beeston Sale Ring.*

58

hold the sales at Beeston. This he gave me without hesitation, and being an Irishman he also generated support from both Eire and Ulster in the months to come. This resulted in a regular Wednesday trip to Manchester Airport to meet prominent horse dealers off the Dublin and Belfast flights at 6.00 am and taxiing them back at night.

The Horse Sales at Beeston became very popular and benefited from the support of many traders from a wide area, including the Gardners from Blackpool; Smiths, from Bedford; Ronnie Mowbray, from Carlisle; Tom Bowdler, from Stafford; Ray Allman, from Madeley, Nr Crewe; and the Wildes, of Mollington, Nr Chester. The Slaughter and Knacker men included Derek Turner, from Bakewell; Potter, from Bristol; Cooper from Sheffield; Warburton, from Knutsford; and Ron Lloyd, from Bronington, Nr Whitchurch. Plus there were those characters that flavour auction marts, typified by Cyril Webb, from Madeley; George Wood, from Leyland; the Maguires, from Wigan; and Joe Beaman, from Brierley Hill, in the West Midlands.

The success of this monthly sale mushroomed. We received a lot of support from Alec Plumley, then of Willington, and the late Fred Wright, of Broxton, who were both very knowledgeable horsemen. However, I didn't realise that you are not able to make a Newmarket out of a Cattle Market! Nevertheless, it became the leading horse sale of its type in the country and many champions in most equine events passed through the Beeston Sale Rings.

My personal interest in equine stock had been confined to the

*Simpsons' Forge, at South Street, Crewe.*
*Simpsons were also local undertakers.*

59

*Judging at the North West & Wales Shire Foal Society Sale,*
*at Beeston Market, in early revival days, in 1978.*

heavy breeds through my early connections at Vine Tree Farm, Wistaston, when it was par for the course if you showed early ability – age was of no consideration! You were soon turned into a field where you progressed from harrowing on pasture and arable to scuffling in roots and turning and tedding in a hay field. Today's safety officers would have turned every farmer into a criminal. The occasional visit to the blacksmith was one of the more tedious tasks when I would have to stand in a queue at the forge in South Street, by Crewe Cattle Market, for anything up to half a day.

*The late Ken Jones, Llanddeusant, Anglesey, exhibiting the Top-priced Shire Foal, 1,450 gns., at Beeston, in 1978. He is receiving the cup from Mrs Kathleen Wright, Whitley Hall.*

So, many years later, it was a pleasure to respond to an approach from Ron Pleavin, of Shordley Manor, Hope, Nr Wrexham, and Arthur Wright, of Whitley Hall, Warrington, to assist in the formation of the North West & Wales Shire Foal Society. The National Shire Foal Society had become defunct and the three of us went to Messrs E.T. Knagg & Sons Solicitors' offices, at Poulton-le-Fylde, Nr Blackpool, to apply for funds for the new society.

There, under the chairmanship of Chris Catterall, a prominent Livestock Haulier from the Fylde, a meeting was held with Mr Baker-Marsh, of Liverpool; Charlie Etches and Tom Yates, of Derby; John Suckley, from Salop; Bill Livesey and Bob Hull, from the Fylde, in attendance. The cups and funds were divided between the existing Midland Foal Society and the newly-formed group. Bob Jones, of Kinsale Hall, North Wales, was another benefactor who, with the respect of all, provided the society with an annual income from his terminal wishes, which included an express desire that I should sell his shire horses... the very last time, in fact, that I picked up the hammer.

The formation of the North West & Wales Shire Foal Society led to the resurrection of the traditional Autumn Foal Sales at Crewe, albeit on a much smaller scale. Through Norman Clare and I, in our capacity as Joint Secretaries to this society, Wright-Manley established strong connections with many of the leading Shire Horse breeders.

*The Wright-Manley Show Dray driven by John Walker with Second Man, Brian Pennington, winning the Turnout Class at Garstang Show, in the early 1980's.*

Subsequently we were favoured with instructions to conduct dispersal sales on behalf of the Executors of such prominent figures as the late Mr Jimmy Walker, of Westhoughton; Mr Lol Heart, of Blackrod, Nr Bolton, in Lancashire; and Mr Bob Jones of Kinsale Hall, Nr Mostyn, in North Wales. Also, the world famous 'Tremoelgoch' Stud, on Anglesey, following the death of the late Mr Gwilym Lloyd-Owen. Other successful Shire Horse Sales were held on behalf of Mr Bob Gardner, at Out Rawcliffe, Nr Blackpool; and, more locally, on behalf of Mr Alistair King, at the Alvanley Arms, Nr Tarporley.

Our involvement in Shire Horse circles eventually led to the acquisition of a Shire Horse Show Dray. This was successfully exhibited at Agricultural Shows in many parts of the UK for several years, in the expert hands of Mr John Walker of Wigan, Lancs. John's success in the Show Ring with Wright-Manley ultimately enabled him to secure a full-time position as Head Horse Man in charge of the Shire Horse Show Dray Team with Messrs Fredric Robinson Ltd., at the Unicorn Brewery, Stockport.

During this peak period of involvement in all these equestrian activities, I was most grateful for the assistance of my youngest daughter, Jane, along with Roger Morris, who were members of staff at that time and undertook many of the administrative duties. Mrs Margaret Clare continued with the secretarial duties at a later date when Jane and Roger had moved on to pursue their careers elsewhere. Roger has since been extremely helpful in formulating this publication.

*Brian Pennington and Roland John*
*at Nantwich Show.*

62

# CHAPTER EIGHT
## Ted Moult and the Tuberculosis Attested Sale

Every effort was now being made to poach an extra customer, particularly if he was a Crewe or Chester man. The majority of Cheshire farms had two important and plentiful commodities to 'dispose of', namely Calves and Barren Cows. The former section was fairly well supported, but the Cull Cow section was very light. To increase entries you needed extra buyers and new buyers would not come without extra cows. So to build up the numbers we benefited from cattle consigned to us by Brian Hancock, Fred Holland and Brian Vaughan, who travelled to other markets throughout the country from Monday to Saturday.

In addition, we were well blessed with the services of many livestock hauliers from a very wide area who, with due respect, are far too numerous to mention individually – to do so would require another chapter. Their invaluable support, which is most gratefully acknowledged, was a crucial factor in developing Beeston into a successful livestock market.

Meanwhile, we had established connections with the abattoirs and meat wholesalers over a very wide area, some well remembered, but only a few remaining in business, eg. the Birtwhistles; John Greenwood and Tom Chadwick, from Bury, Lancashire; Bernard Wharfe and Jim Worsley, from Oldham and Rochdale; Jim Derry and Louis Pollock, from Liverpool; Arthur Proctor from Blackburn; 'Bossy' Laycock , Blackpool; Joe Sykes and Len Moreton, Huddersfield; Jim Arthen, Sheffield; Leylands, of Preston; Gills and Joe Kay, Bolton; Jim and Richard Strange, from Wigan; Ike Powell, Alderley Edge; Alf Coates and Bakers, of Northampton; and Moss Waltham, of Islington London, and many others. These were combined with the emergence of the First Exporters – Frans Buitlaar, Holland; Van Rousse, Belgium, and Albert Cooke, of Crewe, who had attended the same school as myself and he had also broken into the shipping business. The market intelligence so obtained was passed on to our Livestock Trader connections. A good indication of supply and demand was achieved, resulting in better prices than those in our competing markets, and thus we succeeded in our objective to increase throughput.

Calves, on the other hand, were more seasonal in both supply and demand and the calf day at Beeston took place every Monday. However, with the Friday dairy sales improving it became a practice to part the newly-calved beast from its progeny, to maximise price. Amazingly, from the sale of one or two, and without any encouragement or planning by ourselves, over the next eight to ten years the entire calf market moved completely to a Friday.

The Dairy Section was well supported by local traders, including Alan Large, from Sydney, Nr Crewe, who was dealing in those days on his own account; Jack Turner, from Tarvin; and Jim Fellows, of Beeston Sidings, who rewarded the entire office staff with an Annual Christmas Party, at his home. Many local ladies were in attendance, including Miss Pickard, Miss Moors, Mrs Healey, Mrs McCreary, Mrs Young and Miss M. Johnson.

Calf entries were also influenced by a good unloading service for farmers who appreciated our extra efforts as we slowly increased the numbers. The continental demand for the live calf for veal production pushed prices ever higher and Beeston was to become one of the main sources for this and other beef-rearing enterprises, through Albert Halls, of York; Poskitts, of Doncaster; Yarnolds, of Tenbury Wells; Fryatts, of East Anglia; Drinkalls, of Gisburn; and more local buyers, including Ray Ellwood, Arthur Faulkner and Ronny Tomkinson.

The elimination of tuberculosis was being encouraged by the government of the day. Tuberculosis attested herds were gradually being established and we became the first market to have sections for attested and non attested herds which again attracted increased entries, culminating in 1959 with the first 'all attested' stock sale.

We celebrated this milestone in Livestock Health and Welfare by holding a special prize sale in all sections of the Friday Market. We wrote to ask a number of popular celebrities of the time including Dan Archer, of 'The Archers', and others long forgotten, to open the sale and sell the champion dairy cow. All but one replied requesting quite exorbitant fees, which were beyond consideration.

I had given up on the idea when a week or two later I had a telephone call from Ted Moult, at that time one of the 'What's My Line' team on television, which included Gilbert Harding, Barbara Kelly, Dr Isobel Barnett and Eamon Andrews. The conversation went like this:

'Ted Moult speaking, I've been away and have just read your letter. Have you got fixed up?'

Answer, 'No.'

'Oh, would you like me to do it?'

*Ted Moult opens the 'new offices' at Beeston, on October 24th, 1975. Formerly the President's Pavilion at the Royal Lancashire Showground, at Wrea Green, Blackpool. Left to right: Alan and Harold Wright and Brian Pennington witness the occasion.*

Answer, 'Yes please!'

'What sort of a fee should I charge?'

Answer, 'Mr Moult, I have never been engaged in this sort of arrangement before, but the amount of your fee will depend very much upon whether my principals can afford to pay it.' (Bearing in mind previous quotes).

Pause.

'Well I charged twenty pounds to open an egg packing station in West Bromwich last month. How does that sound?'

Answer, 'You're on, I'll confirm it in tonight's post and look forward to meeting you on the due date.'

It was the most successful event ever held at Beeston. The Market was like a race meeting bulging with stock and people. We have had many other successful events since, including the presence of Editors of the Farming Press, public personalities, even a Beauty Queen, Miss Great Britain; MPs and a return by Ted Moult, to open the present offices. But none came quite up to that particular sale, which in my opinion elevated the firm on to a higher plain!

A certain amount of internal rivalry took place due to the fact that Whitchurch Market was also held on Fridays and by now Manleys and Wrights had joined forces at Whitchurch Smithfield. In addition, Beeston was known as an 'afternoon market', waiting for buyers to come from Whitchurch and the train from Crewe, at 2.00 pm, which ruled my starting time on the sale of Cull Cows. It seemed to me that a whole loaf was better than half of one, and I brought the sale time forward three hours to 11.00 am, much to the annoyance of Harold Wright and Cyril Downward. It worked, and we attracted more cows from Shropshire, together with extra buyers.

Success breeds success and if a buyer from a new area came it wouldn't be long before his opposition made an appearance; for example Arthur Green, Jack Longman and Hallets arrived from the Potteries. Another vivid recollection was when the first Barren Cow made £100! Arthur Green who was bidding in the eighties signalled to an accomplice to carry on in order to portray that his interest had ceased. Jack Longman, the opposing bidder who was also very canny, realised the position and called across the ring, 'Pull your ******* dog off Greeny!'

As in most situations where money matters, bitterness often enters the arena and auctioneers need to be very tactful. I recall a situation where I had become 'carried away' and begged for another bid. 'Come again Jack?' thus disclosing the under bidder. It was the same Jack Longman who after the sale pulled me quietly on one side and said, 'When will you grow up?' I had committed the cardinal sin... and learned a very important lesson!

Other men started to attend Beeston regularly such as Tommy Garlick, from Freckleton (North Ribble) and Harry Slinger, from Hesketh Bank (South Ribble), friendly enemies! North Cheshire men included Billy Hollowell, Harry Winstanley, Fred Clarke, Bill Jones and John Hewitt. Amongst the South Lancashire men were Frank Carr, Harry Smith, Jack and Bill Forster, Fred Forshaw, and Tommy Thwaite, who became a very close friend. There were more local men, such as Harry Moore and George Hewitt, and market characters Frank Brereton, of Bridgemere; Alec Furber, of Austerson, and Fred Ellwood, of Oulton Lowe, amongst many others.

The Forster family were the cow merchants of Lancashire and would hold their own 'grading days' at Warrington, St Helens and also Manchester. Amazingly, back in 1939, they had selected Beeston for a sale of imported cattle from Canada. After the war, other feathers were pinned to Joseph Wright's cap when he was instructed to conduct a sale by auction of another importation of Canadian Holsteins, by Messrs Chadwick and Pickering, at the Gorstella, Kinnerton, in 1947.

John and Chris Forster continue in the livestock business, in Lancashire. Brian Hewitt serves the countryside well with a modern slaughter-house at Huxley, Nr Chester. Fred Ellwood's grandson has the largest calf rearing enterprise in the county at Nantwich; whilst Peter Moore and Stan and Edwin Furber still often attend Beeston, on Fridays.

*Robin Arden (left) receives the Joseph Wright Cup, for the Best Dairy Cow, from the Editor of the 'Farmer and Stock Breeder', Mr Harris, watched by Mr Alan Wright.*

Cattle dealers were hard men, and took a lot of handling by young auctioneers. If a bid was missed it took time to restore the relationship, and it had to happen occasionally, as most had their own particular methods of bidding, such as a wriggle of the ear (Jack Forster); a fleeting glance (eyeball to eyeball); a cigarette dropping from a corner of the mouth ('When it is in, I am in; when it is out, I am out'). Tommy Thwaite, a lay preacher, had a more lenient attitude than some, and I quote one of his sayings, 'Never lick the plate clean, Brian, always leave a bit for somebody else.' We were friends for nearly half a century.

One of the many sale ring incidents was when I had supposedly missed a bid from Billy Hollowell who then turned to the successful bidder (a new young client) whilst still looking at the beast with the remark: 'That's cheap young man, buy 'em with a neck like me (a 19-inch collar) and an arse like your mother's and you'll never go far wrong!'

Beeston had always laid claim to the biggest Poultry Sale in the region and was called by some of its critics 'A Cock and Hen Market!' The Monday market attracted poulterers from Liverpool, buying for the Shipping Lines through 'Mac' Macauley, Metcalfe and Butterworth, from Manchester; and Ruben and David Lee, from the kosher trade, at Cheetham Hill, who in times of Fowl Pest would bring with them their own Rabbi, to bless and slaughter on site. Frank Tomlinson, from Broxton, took his first steps to fame and fortune at this time when I loaded him with so many day-old chicks, bought for so little money, that on his way home, along the Whitchurch Road, he had to throw some away over the hedgerow!

The bane of our lives were the Live Christmas Poultry Sales (there were no dressed sales in those days) when thousands of poultry of all

classes arrived at Beeston and the sales would last from early morning until late into the hours of darkness. I recall one particular year when my friend Brian Vaughan had turkeys to sell and I advised him to reserve his pens by placing one bird in each pen on the evening prior to the sale, thus avoiding an early start when most people arrived to claim pens.

Accordingly, we met after the Friday Sale in the Beeston Hotel ready to slip down under cover of darkness at about 10.00 pm, only to find that the Lathams, of Ridley and Chorley, had decided on the same tactic. After a few drinks it was decided that I personally must sell the birds, which filled two whole rows. Trade was so bad on the next day that I failed to sell a feather and the whole exercise proved abortive. I also remember that on the same day, I bought, for 33 shillings, our family bird weighing 36lbs, and that Brian Vaughan had two hen birds left over until the following Christmas when they won first prize.

Experience is a grand tutor and small incidents should be remembered, such as when passing a very critical remark to a casual drover who happened to be a Cockney. He replied, 'All right, all right Sir, we're all God's children you know!' On another occasion when the going happened to be a bit tough at the time, I well remember Andrew

*Before the Canadian Sale at the Gorstella, Chester in 1947, including Mr J. D. Pickering, Mr T. Chadwick and Mr Joseph Wright (centre).*

*Canadian Sale in progress – occupying the rostrum, Mr Joseph Wright, Mr J.D. Pickering and Mr T.D. Henderson.*

Birtwhistle, of Bury, saying to me in his broad Lancashire dialect... 'Brian! You've to be patient. And you've to be realistic!'

There was also an occasion when a farmer approached after the sale with a complaint. 'My cow made £27 and I have only been paid £25:10s!' 'Right Sir, I'll find the buyer.' The buyer insisted £25:10s was the correct figure, but the farmer also insisted that he was right. So next, we found the cow and I asked Fred Holland, of Tiverton, who replied, 'It was either £25 or £26.' Then Tom Holland, from Tattenhall, who replied, 'I put it up at £18 and stuck to it to £25.00's – it made £25:10s.' The farmer still insisted and I dug my heels in. We never saw him again and lost hundreds of pounds in commission. The customer is always right!

Because of similar instances, we ended all future disputes by installing tape recorders to record the auction sales, an example which was quickly followed by many other markets.

There were many men in the livestock business who were phenomenal in their ability to recognise animals that had passed through their hands, or under their scrutiny. They could recognise a particular beast even years later, which was another reason why so few animals were ever stolen. Don Weston, of Stoke-on-Trent, was probably the most outstanding in that ability.

My urban background gradually evaporated as my interest in livestock developed. I found great benefit in furthering my knowledge through practical experience gained by enjoying life as a smallholder, keeping cattle, sheep, pigs and horses. During the course of conducting auction sales, valuations and resolving disputes, this first-hand experience proved to be invaluable.

I first hit the headlines when an Essex sow with a litter of piglets, which belonged to me, was featured on the front cover of the Farmer & Stock Breeder. Then, more recently, as the breeder of the top flight show jumper, 'Wiston Bridget', which has been my greatest claim to fame. Wiston Bridget was sired by David Worthington's Hanovarian Stallion, Rosewal Grandeur, out of a Shire Mare, Garreg Lady Jane, which I purchased as a two-year-old from Mr John Davies, of Garreg Farm, Whitford, near Holywell, in Flintshire.

*The author receives the award for the breeder of the top British Showjumper, at the Horse of the Year Show, 1997. Wiston Bridget has also presented the author with the supreme award for the Best British-bred Showjumper in 2000 and 2001. The rider here is Mr Harvey, of Chesham, Bucks. Wiston Bridget is currently ridden by local man, Tim Stockdale.*

However, this achievement would not have been possible without the kind help of Brian Vaughan, Ted Hollins, from Burleydam, and Geoff Billington, from Coole Pilate, who provided the necessary accommodation and expertise.

Success breeds success and increased entries demand the ability to conduct auction sales with speed, without compromising the price. For that reason, the knock-down price must not be far from the opening bid. The livestock auctioneer needs the co-operation of the buyers in the fatstock rings – which he usually obtains, whilst he needs to apply a similar discipline in the sale rings which have a more flexible price, such as Dairy Cattle, Store Cattle and Calves.

In my prime, I was reputed to have sold 180 cull cows within the hour, but to obtain that rate of sale one requires the back-up of a good droving staff, in particular the 'ring man' who will operate like a robot, knowing exactly when to open and close a gate and to read the auctioneers' requirements like a book. I had the benefit of an experienced Arthur Farrall in the ring and Sid Howell, a Rushton farmer as clerk ... I only needed to pause to draw breath!

The wit of the drovers was also helpful to 'lighten the atmosphere', with comical remarks during the long hours of sale ring battles – always observing the golden rules – 'Behind a Bull' ... and ...

'In front of a Shitter'! (A beast with loose bowels).

The appearance of a new customer at the ringside was an auctioneer's blessing due to the immediate antagonism of the regular buyers. The 'whispers' were often audible from the rostrum:

'Who is he?'

Reply... 'He comes from ....... and he can go a bit!'

'I'll make the ...... go. Is he in?'

A flurry of bids and the new man is the buyer, with a remark from the under bidder...

'Take that old bitch to Water Street and take one and eight for her.'

Water Street was the main Manchester Meat Market, 1s 8d being the price per pound for the dressed carcase.

This situation could only last for a few weeks until everyone realised that a deficit account could not go on indefinitely, and trade would return to a more realistic level.

*Moving to the sale ring in the heydays of the 1980's when thousands of cull cows passed through Beeston, many destined for Europe. Left to right: Tom Thwaite, Liverpool; Billy Swindells, Stockport; Brian Pennington, Brian Vaughan, Nantwich; Frans Buitelaar, Holland; Bill Nield and Brian Hancock, Sandbach.*

# CHAPTER NINE
## Foot & Mouth

By now we had an addition to the ranks through a much needed requirement to fulfil the demand throughout the country for experienced agricultural valuers. This position had been filled by a Welshman named Roland Rosser John. A memorable remark, in the Beeston Castle Hotel, by Edgar Wood, of Beeston Hall was, 'I don't know where he comes from but wherever it is they can grow ****** hair.'

It was all systems go and we were all succeeding in our various departments, until everything came to a sudden halt when the worst ever outbreak of Foot & Mouth disease in Cheshire restricted all movement of animals in October 1967!

The first Foot & Mouth valuations were undertaken in tandem by Harold Wright and myself and Alan Wright and Tommy Henderson. In a matter of days we were working round the clock until, after two or three weeks, the team had to be increased and eventually there were seven of us including Roland John, Cyril Downward and John Broomhall. I had a small farm at Betley at this time and was asked by the Head Veterinary Surgeon to leave home if I was to continue as a valuer. I complied with his request, returned home for Christmas lunch and was called out to a case on King Street, Middlewich, which brought my Christmas celebrations to a sudden end. And I eventually returned home in March of the following year! Lots of words have been written about Foot & Mouth, which affected

*One of the smaller outbreaks of Foot & Mouth Disease, in 1953. Picture shows a local coalman, forbidden to enter Brook House, Wettenhall, tipping over the roadside wall for Mr Niel Kinsey, right.*

*The 1967/68 Foot & Mouth epidemic struck over 1,000 Cheshire farmers. Over 90,000 cattle, 16,000 sheep and 42,000 pigs were slaughtered.*

all farms, and everybody connected with agriculture for nearly twelve months; and cattle markets were closed as a result.

As restrictions were lifted, auction sales resumed, but Beeston, being at the heart of the plague, was the last market to re-open. This gave us the opportunity to think about the steps we should take in continuing to improve on the foundations we had established. So we decided to visit Ireland, which had remained free of the disease, with a view to arranging sales of Irish cattle at Beeston, to replace the depleted herds. On a previous visit to Ireland, I had been very impressed by the weighing of store cattle at the point of sale and was keen to introduce the system into Beeston. With this in mind I contacted the manager of Ulster Farmers Limited, a man named Johnston,

*Brian Pennington, Alan Wright and Brian Robson discussing the situation in an empty Beeston Market, in 1953.*

73

who had approached me twenty years previously to work for him in Portadown; and also the manager of Ganley's Auction, in Dublin, for similar arrangements in the Free State.

As a result Harold, Alan and I travelled to Belfast where we were lucky to be able to pass through strict agricultural security by virtue of one inspector who turned a blind eye to our known background with a wink in the other. He had, by coincidence, been engaged with the Ministry in Cheshire during the epidemic and we had come to know him well via the Badger Inn, at Church Minshull, Nr Nantwich.

Purpose fulfilled with Mr Johnston, we travelled by train to Dublin, booked in at the Gresham Hotel with a view to making similar arrangements for tours of farms in the South. After unloading the cases we toured some of Dublin's bars and returned to the Gresham to be met by a posse of officials from the Irish Agricultural Ministry.

The new Store Cattle ring, which replaced the Poultry Shed, was fitted with platform weighbridge, complete with digital display and duplicated, as seen here for the sale, by Mr Alan Wright, of Fat Cattle in single lots. Digital display – Lot No. 35. Weight 7 cwt. 3 qrts.

They were astounded that we had gained entry to the Emerald Isle and forbade us to move outside the hotel. However, we had useful conversations with our Dublin counterparts and returned home reasonably happy. I had intended to show Harold and Alan the Store Cattle sales but they took my word for it and we started to convert the Poultry Shed at Beeston into a Store Cattle Market with a platform weighbridge. During this time we decided to improve on the Irish version by incorporating electronically controlled, digital displays and visited markets in the south of England, which were already using the system for Fat Cattle.

It was on our return from one of these trips that we became marooned, along

74

with hundreds of others, at Newcastle-under-Lyme, in Staffordshire, during a freak snowstorm when the M6 was closed. Harold Wright slept in the car while Alan and I slept on the floor with scores of others at the Castle Hotel, which had benevolently opened its doors to the refugees! At about 1.00 am a young couple who lay beside me could resist no longer to the call of love and an act of gross indecency was commenced under the blanket provided by the hotel. I refused for reasons of either envy, or disgust, to witness the matter further and made more space available by making my way to the kitchen. Alan, who always possessed a more placid nature, had a good night's sleep and failed to witness this embarrassing event!

The next step was to find a suitable auctioneer for the Store Cattle section. John Broomhall by this time had established himself as a very capable young man in the rostrum and the arrangements were in place to attract the Dairy and Beef Cross Store Cattle from Cheshire and further afield.

John swelled his weekly numbers through his services to many extra buyers and sellers from ever extending areas through Tony Jones, of St Martins, and the Tomley family, of Gobowen, in Shropshire; Tom Owen, of Widnes, and his cousin Geoff Webster, from St Helens; Ray Woods and the Philbins, of Wigan, in Lancashire; the

*Joseph Wright's head office moves from the family home at Alpraham to Tarporley to be officially opened by the firm's oldest client, Mr Charlie Hopley, of Tattenhall Lanes. Left to right: John Broomhall, Noel Guest, Sam Basford, Ray Walker, Rosemary Miller, Frank Wilson, Tom Henderson, Alan Wright, Harold Wright, Harry Watson and Brian Pennington.*

Holgates and Metcalfes, of Yorkshire; and Cyril Moss, from North Staffs. Whilst the Hancocks, of Sandbach, who have now traded with the firm for four generations, were able to obtain their requirements for an ever expanding business from a local source.

John's appointment as Chairman of the famous Nantwich Show also provided him and, ultimately, the company, with valuable connections, and its spin-off was to the advantage of a firm continuing to improve its services and boost its popularity. The result was that Beeston had become successful in all departments, which had the desired effect on other centres.

Reflecting on the idea of weighing Store Cattle we decided to introduce the idea to the Cull Cow section. This had been tried in one other market and failed through lack of support as it was traditional to sell per head. We decided to run the two methods side by side, at the option of the vendor. In a very short period of time the percentage weighed moved from 5% to 95%, and at the same time attracted increased entries from much further afield.

*The late Charlie Hopley who, in the late 1940's/early 1950's, would drive about 40 Coloury Roan Yearling Heifers from Tattenhall to Beeston, to the Spring Prize Store Stock Sales, and invariably would take first prize.*

By now the firm had established a broad base and increased the number of branch offices involved in Estate Agency and Property Valuation. To quote Harold Wright's words to me, in company with Alan, 'Brian, the firm has become too big for us to manage on our own, and we would like to take you into partnership. It will cost you £X for X shares.'

It was entirely unexpected and I was quite overwhelmed when Alan in his usual cautious manner said, 'Go home and think about it!', to which I replied, 'I don't need to think about it!'. I paid the required sum shortly afterwards. Of course, invitations had also been extended to Tommy Henderson, Roland John, Cyril Downward and Jack Burningham, and the first partnership was, therefore, formed. A team of people with different qualities had come together, all with a special contribution to make and the firm's progress continued at a rapid pace.

At this stage, the reader may care to reflect on the advances in methods of accounting over the past thirty years, which in market terms used to be very labour intensive. Our original offices at Beeston were old, crude and poorly furnished without any form of effective heating! The working day began between 7.00 and 8.00 am and, in addition to rostrum duties, we filled in on any staff shortages prior to sale times and concluded with office work after the sales had ended.

The system of balancing the books in those early days was as antiquated as the building we worked in. It was rare that we struck a first time balance, and equally as rare that we were able to end the day's work before 7.00 pm - in fact it was quite often 10.00 pm! However, the arrival of the computer, in the 1980's completely revolutionised our accounting systems. After a transitional period of hard work under the dedicated leadership of Alan Wright, our Market Accounts became fully computerised! A late finish at the end of the day became a thing of the past; and everybody was able to go home at a sensible hour.

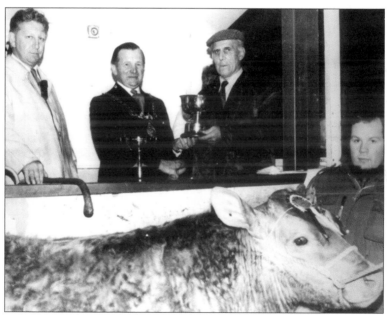

*Beeston Fatstock Champion in the 1970's, left to right: B. Pennington; Mr Mitchell, Farmer of Christleton and Mayor of Chester; Mr Cooper, Coal Merchant and Farmer, Kingsley; and buyer, Mr Dutton, Butcher, Kelsall.*

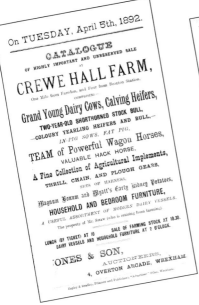

## SATURDAY, 18th MAY, 1968

at 10.30 a.m. prompt

**Highly Important Agricultural Dispersal Sale**

at

## CREWE HALL FARM

FARNDON, Nr. CHESTER

briefly comprising :

# 94

### Choice Dehorned

# FRIESIAN DAIRY COWS HEIFERS & YOUNG STOCK

3 DIESEL TRACTORS
REPLETE RANGE OF FARM EQUIPMENT
POULTRY HOUSES : BARN MACHINERY
SURPLUS HOUSEHOLD FURNITURE

Auctioneers :

## JOSEPH WRIGHT

who have been favoured with instructions from Mr. T. E. Appleby
to conduct this sale.

Auctioneers' Offices :

62 Northgate Street, Chester ............... Tel. 28028
16 Watergate Street, Whitchurch ...,.... Tel. 2281/2/3
Alpraham, Tarporley ............... Tel. Bunbury 467/8
Also at Winsford and Nantwich.

Changing fortunes at Crewe Hall Farm, Farndon. The first sale, in 1892, realised £1,100 and included a 'team of powerful wagon horses', as well as cattle, implements and furniture. The sale in 1937, conducted by Leonard Wright & Co., included dairy cattle, pig herd, poultry and antique and modern furnishings. Horse-power was then still predominant; the top price, for a bay shire mare, 17 hands, was £54. Twelve two-year-old shorthorn heifers fetched £204 and the overall sale realised £2,400. The 1968 sale, for Mr T.E.Appleby, came under the hammer of Joseph Wright. The central feature of some 350 lots was a Friesian dairy herd, 'all home-bred'.

The livestock market business was probably more vulnerable to bad debts than any other form of commerce, and it was an accepted situation that a previously unknown face would appear at the ringside without any credentials and bid freely. The only surety available would be obtained from one or more regular patrons with assurances such as, 'I've seen him at such and such a market and I've heard nowt wrong!' By this time he would have spent hundreds of pounds. The plus side was that Mr X had improved the trade which had resulted in higher prices than our competitors and we often thought that the risk was worth taking. In any case, the word of a bank manager was not very valuable, or reliable, particularly when he wanted his client to obtain sufficient means of solvency to balance the account and enable the bank to close it on the following day!

When the market grapevine failed, it often proved an unwritten obligation that I should be classed as the 'Head Debt Collector!', a task which I detested, but one at which I achieved a fair measure of success. The first essential was to appear on the debtor's doorstep no later than 6.30 am when his wits were at their lowest point. It was essential to be ruthless and lose all sense of sentiment and, where necessary, acquire 'The complete assets of the establishment' and remove them as quickly as possible. They were often fools rather than frauds, the latter performing premeditated swindle or credit abuse, which have been the scourge of the livestock auction business!

Having said that, the main core of buyers in every department were honest, trustworthy men; a breed of their own, well blessed with wit and humour. Cattle dealing was a tradition in some families such as the Westons from the Leek area in Staffordshire, who specialised in the Cull Cow sections. They would pride themselves on 'standing their corner' and buy literally hundreds of cows, not knowing what to do with them at the time and then retire to the market pub!

Whatever the situation the following morning they would appear at the ringside of their market of the day, immaculate in appearance, ready to battle and do business come what may ... fortunes won and lost along the way. Another branch of the Weston family, from Stoke-on-Trent, were also well known characters in the 'Calf Rings'. I am sure that the Equal Rights' section of the female gender would never have been in contest!

# CHAPTER TEN
## Across the Dee and the Mersey

During this period the Partnership was very keen to expand into Chester territory and so we approached a young Scot who had made a recent impact at Chester Market, to persuade him to transfer his loyalties. This was the reversal of a situation which had happened some years previously, when I had been approached, and virtually accepted, a position at Chester, only to be persuaded, via a substantial increase in salary, to remain at Beeston. No doubt, the young Scot was retained through similar negotiations. Not to be thwarted we persuaded Roland John to occupy a rented office in Chester and thereby established the first foot on 'enemy territory'. Roland through his expertise in agricultural law expanded the foothold, which helped the amalgamation that followed.

In another attempt to cross the Rivers Dee and Mersey, I had a revolutionary idea to acquire Liverpool Livestock Market which was held at Stanley Abattoir.

## Record prices revealed in trade preview

RECORD prizes for cull cows, sows and store pigs highlighted an exceptional trading year at Beeston and Chester Livestock Markets during 1977, according to the annual review of trade published this week by the livestock auctioneers, Wright and Partners.

Prices for cull cows reached more than £400 and sows and litters topped £200 at peak periods. And for the first time in the 100 year history of Beeston Castle Market a price of over £600 was recorded for cows and heifers during the October sales.

Wright and Partners anticipate a further escalation of prices this year for store cattle in particular, with continued increases also for fat cattle. Calf prices are expected to remain at present levels although there could be an improvement later in the year, while a firm trade should continue for cull cows and brucellosis accredited dairy cows.....

*Chronicle,*
*January 1978*

The ideology behind the thought was to take the stock to the buyers and maximise value at the point of slaughter. My friend, Tommy Thwaite's family were the owners and, fortunately in retrospect, asked too high a price and, eventually, the sales petered out.

Meanwhile, Chester Market had suffered in various ways, including an ageing partnership under Leonard Wright, a town centre market, the effect of our success at Beeston and also the encroachment of development at the expense of agriculture on the Wirral. As a result, the partners of Leonard Wright & Co. had either retired or

*The partners of Joseph Wright and Leonard Wright & Co, back row, l-r, Robert Brown, John Minshull, Cyril Downward, Jack Burningham, Roland John. Front row: Tommy Henderson, Alan Wright, Harold Wright and Brian Pennington.*

passed away, including, after Leonard himself, some very fine professionals in Mr Les Foster, Chris Mills, and Frank Tranter, whilst others with lesser interests were Harold Green, the cashier who had withdrawn to a salaried post, leaving two young men, Robert Brown and John Minshall.

They were finding their positions hard going and saw the benefits of amalgamation. Hence, Joseph Wright and Leonard Wright & Co. was eventually formed. They in turn had seen the demise of Frodsham and Hooton Markets and saw the joint venture as a means of prolonging Chester as a Livestock Marketing Centre in a proposed move to Sealand.

Chester City Council had decided to build a new market at Sealand to fit into the new road systems and Industrial Estates. So, for the first time, the Livestock Market moved out of the city and we transferred to Bumpers Lane where the New Market was opened by Lord Woolley, in 1972.

By now our 'Senior Partner', Tommy Henderson, had reached OAP status which was never ever reflected in either looks or effort. It seemed to me a sad situation that he had to leave the partnership at such an early stage after making such a sterling contribution and before the full benefits of the partnership had been achieved.

He was replaced by John Broomhall who had taken the baton in

81

promoting the Store Cattle section at Beeston, which was the first market in the UK to weigh stores at the point of sale; and coupled with his efforts became the leading store market in the North West. John, having been with the firm from leaving school, had been moulded in the same conditions as the rest of us, and so the partnership retained the 'status quo'.

Before the common use of microphones at an affordable price, there was a rather stubborn attitude by most livestock auctioneers against their use, and a sense of pride, or conceit, in being able to be easily heard without one. In any case, you were never considered suitable for the rostrum without a strong voice, particularly in view of the fact that in the early days, an auctioneer required a licence, which carried a fee of £100 per annum.

Meanwhile, Beeston had established itself as the biggest Cull Cow centre in Great Britain. Selling six days per week had taken its toll, and my voice box needed surgery. The need for a replacement in the Dairy Cattle Rostrum following Mr Henderson's retirement offered a less demanding role. The Dairy section, having been his pride and joy, had received his meticulous attention, as he had applied his energies to every other aspect of the business. Here he had been very ably assisted by Ray Walker who had joined the firm from Gandy & Sons, the Northwich-based Land Agents. Ray remained a popular member of staff in the Dairy Cattle section at Beeston for many years, until his retirement in 2001.

As a result, I needed to maintain good relations with valuable clients, such as Tom Berrisford, of Endon, Stoke-on-Trent; Mr Mosley, Matlock; Tom Campbell, Cheadle, Staffs; Mr Sadler, Whitefield, Manchester; Jim Atkinson, Barrowford, Lancs, together with a long-

*The 'new offices' at Beeston, opened in 1975.*

established connection in North Wales, namely Mr Tom Eyton-Jones, of Ruthin. Not to forget the longest connection of all, Jack Lakin of Church Minshull who is still at Beeston aged ninety four! Special entries of lying off calvers from specialist grazers, like the Webbs, of Plumley, along with herd dispersals and reductions, were a regular feature.

*Norman Clare (right) replaced Roland John (left) in the partnership in 1984.*

Grapevines exist in every aspect of life and it had reached us that Norman Clare was not happy at Crewe. I had known Norman from when he had joined the staff at Manley's, in 1947, and we considered him to be the ideal man to carry on the good work in the Cull Cow section at Beeston. Accordingly, he was headhunted and joined us on August 1st, 1974. Norman's subsequent efforts were ultimately rewarded in his appointment as a partner of Wright-Manley in 1983.

The Council's decision to build the New Market, on the west side of Chester, had been privately welcomed by us and had taken place prior to the amalgamation. The effect of the move was fairly predictable, in that the staunch Chester supporters from the districts south and east of the city turned slowly to Beeston. But contrary to many opinions, this was never encouraged in my time as Senior Market Partner. On the contrary, it was of prime importance to attract as much stock as possible to cover the high rent exceeding £50,000 per annum - just a start of the money required to fund the operation of the new market!

For the first time we now had strong links with North Wales and the Wirral and the benefit of the continued custom of such stalwarts in

*Miss Great Britain, Pat Morgan, presents the prizes at the annual Dairy Cattle stock show at Beeston, watched by Eryl Cadwaladr, Alan Wright and Judges, Mr Dobson, of Shrewsbury, and Tony Kirkham, of Ridley.*

83

the cattle trade as Tom Dawson, from Buckley, John Dawson, from Hope and Glyn Williams & Son, from Saughall. Those who had patronised both markets under separate heads helped our steady progress, and in particular the Cadwaladr family whose guidance by now had fallen to Eryl, the eldest son of Tommy who was, possibly, one of the cattle trade's most colourful characters, an ex-publican who

*Sheep buyers in action at Chester.*

*John Minshall turns business into laughter, an ability with which he was well blessed. Tom Owen is obviously enjoying the remarks as much as he took pleasure in exhibiting many Xmas fatstock champions in markets throughout the North West over many years.*

*Auctioneer, Roger Morris in action. Also in the picture are: John Pinnington, John Jones, Tarvin; John Gosmore, Tattenhall; Ron Blake, Malpas; John Williamson, Willington; Harry Winstanley, Stretton; John Lightfoot, Kingsley etc..*

could lay claim to being on good terms with everybody in the North West and Wales connected with either agriculture, alcohol or both! His famous song to a lilting melody goes:

### Cadwaladr's Cows
If they're Blues or Blacks or Whites
They're Cadwaladr's Cows.
If they walk with a bit of a swing,
The Old Cheshire Farmer
Says they're just the thing.
They touch so silky and draw so milky
They are Cadwaladr's Cows.

....which Tommy sang with great gusto in market bars all over the country!

The Chester Sales were supplemented by a good percentage of casual staff, taken from inner city positions on market days, with names like Hooky Lewis, Trousers, Whizzo, etc., all market characters in their own right, recruited by the 'Market Foreman' Charlie Hignett, who combined his market duties with that of Commission Agent, by acting for many buyers who were unable to attend in any section of the market. The Department of Employment was also making inroads into systems of casual employment and forced our hand under threat

85

of heavy penalty to obtain full details of these personnel. This I attempted following the end of one market day and, as a result, without warning we had to conduct the next market minus the casual staff. They had disappeared into the woodwork and were never seen again!

Objective number one had been achieved, having established our foothold into Chester primarily as a result of the devoted efforts of seven keen young men. By the same reasoning, the opposing firms had failed to introduce younger partners with the same vitality to arrest the decline in business until it was too late, and there was little alternative but to amalgamate. We had now acquired two more market days at Chester, which put us in a position of being able to hold a market on every day of the week, and I had been entrusted with the responsibility of making the necessary arrangements, now with the valuable assistance of John Minshall and Robert Brown (with whom I am pleased to say I forged a comparatively short but very pleasant personal and working relationship, terminated by John's decision to move south and Robert's premature death).

As with every new building, Chester market was designed to eliminate the problems of the older ones and, by and large, succeeded. One exception was that it was illuminated like a theatre, which added to the expense of a formidable rent requiring a 'full house' on every market day. Most farmers from the Wirral and the banks of the Dee Estuary supported the new venture. A good haulage service was provided by family businesses from the Wirral, North Wales and South Lancashire.

We had also inherited some good 'buying power' from local farmers who supplied the meat trade and the requirements of the

*Six 'Old' Drovers. l-r: Joe Martin, Frank Hough and four of the Farrall family, Jim, Arthur, Tom and Mike, the sole survivor.*

*The Team – Back Row (l-r): John Bowen, Wilf Belcher, Roger Morris, Andrew Wallace, Alan Muskett, Clive Norbury, Steven Welch, Graham Martyn, David Fisher, Chris Stokes, Philip Venner.*
*Front Row (l-r): John Broomhall, Norman Clare, Brian Pennington, Alan Wright, Geoff Moss.*

larger farms through Harry and, latterly, Peter Moore, from Vicars Cross; the Latham family, Pipers Ash; Neville Bellis, Buckley; John Goulding, Puddington; Harry Southern, Wirral; and Roy Shaw, of Mollington, whose diverse interests once gave me the privilege to offer, from the rear of an articulated lorry, a record quantity of tinned strawberries – one of the largest bulk food sales ever to take place in a cattle market.

We had by this time increased our marketing staff and formed a good team of hard working young men including Roger Morris, from Llanarmon-yn-Iâl, who spoke the Welsh language fluently and proved

*The first Park and Ride service in the city featuring*
*John Minshall and Peter Dainty.*

to be an excellent connection in North Wales. I well remember his reply when attempting to squeeze an extra bit of effort from him to attract entries from the Mold and St Asaph areas ... 'It's getting 'em over that Queensferry Bridge, Mr Pennington!'

Nevertheless, we had a good support from North Wales and it was not long before we introduced 'walkie-talkies', a two-way telephone system – the first mobile phones – to control the queues which extended from the market entrance to the Sealand Road. A little before our time perhaps, but we also started a bus service to and from the city centre to the market for the benefit of our 'farmer's wives' ... the very first attempt in the city to Park and Ride!

Despite all our efforts and the modern facilities at Chester, including restaurant and bar facilities, plate glass windows and entrance halls, we were never able to make Chester as busy as Beeston. I well remember an incident at the first sale when due to the fact that it was difficult to discern the beginning of a door and the end of a window, Harry Smith, from Burscough, hammered on the glass panels asking in his inimitable broad Lancashire accent, 'How do ah git troo to Twaitey?' – Tommy Thwaite was in the cafe eating his lunch!

Our overall success had obvious repercussions on other markets, including Crewe, and we did not have too long to wait before discussions were to take place, with a view to amalgamation, with Henry Manley & Sons Ltd., through their new chairman, John Pywell.

And so in 1979, as in 1900, when Manley's had absorbed its competition, Wright's repeated the operation and, in doing so, acquired the expertise to cover every aspect of livestock marketing. As a result,

*Chester Cull Cow Ring – Auctioneers Norman Clare
and Brian Pennington.*

88

the original partnership of Harold and Alan Wright had now been increased to include Brian Robson, Bill Duff and Horace Stokes, ie two to thirteen, John Bourne and Tom Jefferson having retired.

We were now in the fortunate position of having a good team of auctioneers; a market office staff under Noel Guest, Harold Green and Harry Watson, and a droving workforce under Arthur Farrall, whose family must have totalled 150 years' service at Beeston.

With three markets to manage it was a logical step to convert each centre into a one-day market in order to streamline the business, to eliminate internal competition and to maximise the use of the staff and improve profitability. Consequently, a weekly market schedule was introduced commencing with combined weekly sales of all classes of stock at Crewe, on a Monday; Chester, on a Tuesday; and Beeston, on a Friday. Horse Sales and Implement Sales filled the Wednesday slot, which left Thursdays and Saturdays available for private dispersal sales and market maintenance.

In addition, thanks to the initiative of John Minshall, prior to his departure, we were also responsible for the broadcast of the Farming Reports on Marcher Sound, the local radio station based at Gwersyllt, between Mold and Wrexham, in North Wales. These daily reports complemented the production of our 'Weekly Market News' publication that was always in popular demand throughout the region, which now extended from Caerwys across to Congleton, and from Wigan down to Walsall.

It was a hard relentless week. Excellent connections over a wide rural area were of benefit to every department of the expanded firm. Prior to these arrangements when the sales at Crewe and Beeston were held on the same day, I was travelling between the two markets when the traffic police detained me outside Nantwich Barony Hospital. It was no help when a raucous voice from an old drover, Fred Woolley, sitting on the institute wall yelled, 'Lock him up officer – he never was any good!' I was referred to, from then on, by our droving staff as 'Pennington, The Speed King!'

There was some dissension within the partnership when we decided to hold only one Christmas Fatstock Show to cover the three markets and Crewe was selected as the most suitable venue, but its immediate success as an evening event proved the point. Naturally, this did not meet with everyone's approval and, understandably so, when you informed men who had attended their own individual market for a lifetime on a certain day. We were not very popular and suffered a temporary setback, but over time we were forgiven.

89

*The Champion in the first combined sale, exhibited by Sharon Plant, of Leek, and purchased by John Pennington, in business at that time as a Butcher in Winsford. From left to right: the Mayor of Crewe; Alan Wright, Chairman; Wright-Manley; Sharon Plant; John Pennington; David Potts; and, on the extreme right, Mr John Vernon, Tattenhall, who held a record of purchasing stock from the Xmas Sales for forty consecutive years.*

*The Xmas Fatstock Show, at Crewe, in 1993, l-r, Harry Clewlow, Butcher, Nantwich; Michael Mulliner, Judge and Wholesale Butcher; Mrs Barbara Smith, Chairperson, Cheshire WFU; John Lewis, the current Chairman of Wright-Manley; and the winner, David Hancock, Elton, Sandbach.*

90

*The Market News, of September 13th 1985, showing John Broomhall in the weekly Fat Cattle rostrum, at Crewe. This magazine was very popular and although it was free, it was almost always a 'sell out' and provided good information on all market and farming matters.*

# CHAPTER ELEVEN
## The end of the beginning and the need to change course

*Cups and Prizes for competition at the first Xmas Fatstock Show and Sale to be held in the evening, and also the first sale which combined the three centres into one event. Held at Crewe in 1985, it included sausage-making competitions and classes for the Women's Institute, organised by Mrs M.Shufflebottom.*

Since I started to write the first words of this small piece of farming history, the prediction, which I have held for many years, of the rationalisation of Livestock Markets has been brought forward at amazing speed by the recent BSE and latest Foot & Mouth epidemics.

Added to this has been the passing of two more former partners, namely Harold Wright and Roland John. I, therefore, decided that the final chapters had to be completed before some human epidemic obliterated my ability, or my Divine Licence was withdrawn!

The original partnerships had benefited from the energies of the young and the added demise of the firms who had neglected to introduce new blood into management and also to acquire, and foster, younger talent within the staff. Brian Robson had acquired great knowledge and skill in the Pedigree Livestock Department and also recruited a protégé in Clive Norbury, whom he trained and imparted valuable guidance to during his formative years. When Brian took early retirement, Clive was a ready-made successor. Through his own efforts, along with the help of Norman Clare who had also been closely connected with the Pedigree Department during his thirty years with Manley's, the old adage 'Have gavel – will travel' was raised, and the national image was resurrected. They also benefited from the loyal service of David Briggs and Julie Latham, who both worked in the Department for a lifetime.

Graham Martyn, who had been imported from the South West, the son of a Cornish farmer, became an excellent successor to Tommy Henderson and Roland John, through his

*Beeston Market has provided a permanent home for Bill Witter to establish furniture and fine art sales which have developed from the market hall auctions at Whitchurch, Wem, Nantwich and Northwich.*

qualifications and agricultural expertise, coupled with his ability and adaptability to the requirements of a Livestock Market.

Andrew Wallace, who grew up in the shadow of Beeston, has also

*Malcolm Brunton, Resident Yardsman for 30 years outside The Cottage at Beeston entrance. This is the only surviving building from the original market.*

93

developed into an excellent Livestock Auctioneer and Agricultural Valuer, having recently re-established Beeston as the leading Calf Market in Great Britain.

Other successful heads of firms who have passed through our market cloisters, include Roger Griffiths, head of the family firm of J. Bradburne Price & Co., at Mold, in North Wales; and Richard Morris, Managing Director of Penrith Farmers' & Kidds plc, whilst others who established their own firms within the profession include Robert Windsor, Robert Ikin and Geoffrey Elson.

Left deliberately to the end is John Lewis, the present Senior Partner, who was selected to succeed Alan Wright over ten years ago. John was plucked from his Shropshire roots in 1973 and was made a

*A reunion of retired partners is held each year at a local hotel. The photograph above includes, l-r: the late Tom Henderson, the late Roland John, Brian Robson, Alan Wright, the late Harold Wright, Brian Pennington, Bill Duff and Norman Clare.*

*The photograph below, in 2001, shows, l-r: Bill Duff, John Broomhall, Brian Robson, Brian Pennington, Alan Wright, Cyril Downward, and Norman Clare.*

partner in 1980. His excellent agricultural knowledge, ably supported by his professional qualifications, was further enhanced by his outstanding attitude to hard work. He, therefore, stood out as the ideal replacement for grooming to his current position. Since his inception, agriculture has been subject to the most rigorous reforms in its history. Yet John and his partners have moved in the right direction and made substantial investments in the continued development of Beeston Livestock Market which is now one of the most up-to-date premises in the country. It is now able to serve the requirements of the Livestock Farmers over regions far wider than the founders could ever have envisaged!

Nevertheless, I feel sure these founders would have been pleased that the family connections are still maintained, through to the present partnership in which Paul Wright (Joseph Wright's great-grandson), and Miles Lewis (John's son) work in tandem with Nigel Eckersley, who oversees a very successful Estate Agency, consisting of five branch offices at Chester, Tarporley, Crewe, Whitchurch and Nantwich. The Manley family connection ended with the retirement of Mr Bill Duff, in 1990.

## ... and finally

The demise of the small slaughter-house, the power of the supermarkets, and the elimination of the small farmer, has obvious reflections on the number of livestock auction markets required to service the industry. However, the continued presence of the auction system is essential in order to eliminate the possibility of the monopoly of direct sales, with too much emphasis on form-filling and too little on producer returns. The open market is still the yardstick and barometer to safeguard against that situation.

By today, many of the livestock auctioneers featured in the earlier chapters of this book have either passed away, or retired. However, I feel sure that I speak for them all when I say that life was always a balancing act between buyer and seller; the righteous and the rogue; the shrewd and the silly. Yet if we made some contribution to rural life in the twentieth century, all our efforts will have been well worthwhile.

*The 2002 Wright-Manley Partnership. Back (left to right): Miles Lewis, Clive Norbury, Graham Martyn. Front: Paul Wright, John Lewis, Nigel Eckersley.*